MW01231926

Publish and be damned
www.pabd.com

The Whispering Heart

Your Inner Guide To Creativity

How to unlock your creative power, turn dreams into
reality and live with joy

Shannon Skinner

Publish and be damned
www.pabd.com

Copyright © 2005 by Shannon Skinner

All rights reserved. This book, or parts thereof, may not be reproduced in any form without written permission from the publisher.

Published by Comfy Chair Productions Inc.
880 Broadview Ave., Suite #3
Toronto, Ontario CANADA   M4K 2R1
Tel. 416-405-8809
www.comfychairproductions.com

ISBN 0-9737615-0-4

Editorial: Sherman Adams
Cover Design: Dianne Semark
Text Design: Andreas Duess
www.düss.com

First Edition: May 2005

Distributed by Publish and be damned, Toronto, Canada
www.pabd.com

Publish and be Damned helps writers publish their books with absolutely no set-up costs or publishing fees. The service uses a series of automated tools to design and print your book on-demand, eliminating the need for large print runs and inventory costs.
Now, there's nothing stopping you getting
your book into print quickly and easily.

**For more information or to visit our bookstore
please visit us at www.pabd.com**

To my mentor, Dr. Lise Janelle, whose *Inward Bound* seminar on self-worth, the seven areas of life, and listening to the wisdom of one's heart is, in part, the basis for some of the guiding principles in this book. Lise, my deepest gratitude for teaching me how to open my whispering heart, your invaluable guidance on the manuscript and for inspiring me every step of the way.

Looking at the stars always makes me dream.
-- Vincent van Gogh

Acknowledgements

I wish to thank my friend Sherman Adams for helping me get the right words on paper, and for your patience and loving support over the years. And heartfelt thanks to Dianne Semark for designing the book cover that touches my heart every time I pick it up, and for your friendship that means so much to me.

I also wish to acknowledge Cubby Coatsworth, Jim Hawtin, Martyn Schmoll and Kirsten Andrews. And special thanks to Andreas Duess with *Publish and be damned,* for your professional advice and generous assistance in helping get this book "out there."

I thank my parents, Leigh and Darlene Skinner, for your unending love and support, and for creating me in the first place. I also wish to thank the rest of my family for being a family through thick and thin.

And last, but not least, thank you to my many friends for opening your hearts and for your words of encouragement over the years.

Gratitude is the heart's memory.
-- French proverb

Contents

Introduction

The pursuit of truth and beauty is a sphere of activity
in which we are permitted to remain children all our lives.
-- Albert Einstein

Dreams Are the Gems of Creativity

Ahh, yes…*The Dream.*
The dream is the heartbeat of the human spirit. It gives birth to new ideas, different ways of thinking, adventures, innovation, career opportunities, art, music, loving relationships, wealth, success, and lives filled with joy and meaning.

Dreaming has given us medical breakthroughs, space walks, the Olympics, the Eiffel Tower, radio, television, movies and books that have stood the test of time. We are able to talk to each other over the telephone from nearly any place on earth because of a dream. World leaders have founded movements and mobilized the masses based on a dream.

The dream has birthed awe-inspiring masterpieces from Leonardo da Vinci, Michelangelo, Mozart, Chopin, Shakespeare, Jane Austen, Fellini, Renoir, Humphrey Bogart, Marlene Dietrich and Louis Armstrong.

Behind every dream is a creative mind. And dreams are the precious gems of creativity.

I assume the reason you picked up this book is because you have a desire to be more creative. Perhaps you feel it is time to pursue a creative dream that has teased you for ages, but you are not certain where or how to begin. Or you have a vision of a way of life you long for, but a spell of self-doubt holds you back from taking action steps to make it happen.

Well, do not fret. You are surely not alone.

The spirit of the dream keeps us moving forward in life. We *all* have ideas, aspirations and goals, whether it is the desire to create a new product or service, the ultimate job, art, or simply a better way of living. Like each perfect snowflake that is designed like no other, you are unique in your design -- in all of the history of creation. So

11

are your dreams. There is no other human who shares your blend of intelligence, biochemistry, skills, talents, memories and personality quirks -- sprinkled with dreams. *Your dreams, whatever you wish or desire to bring into this world throughout your lifetime, are the precious gems of your creativity.*

If you take a look at the people around you, you will probably see that most of them dream of creating something special. Some of those people probably pursue their heart's desires. However, chances are nearly all of these people are held back from being fully creative and making their dreams happen. The question is *why*?

Brett, a former colleague, works as a copywriter at an advertising agency, but he has a deep desire to be an author. He has never pursued his dream because the security of his job is too comfortable to take the risk of not paying the bills. My friend Laura dreams of starting a catering business, but says her high paying job as an executive in a corporation is too lucrative to give up for the uncertainty of whether she could earn a living from a new business venture. Shelley, another woman I know, dreams of being a painter and courageously left her day job to pursue it, but the worry of not making ends meet forced her to give up the canvases and go back to the comforts of employment.

Each of them knows what is in their heart, but rather than stepping outside their zone of comfort to follow their desire, something keeps them stuck. That something is an obstacle.

The only thing between you and *your* dream is nothing more than *an obstacle in your mind*. The good news is, with some invaluable tools and a little elbow grease, these obstacles can be identified and removed. And then you can unlock your creative power and bring to life anything you wish.

At this point you may be wondering if this book is for you. Well, let's see…

- Does worry stop you from pursuing a new skill?
- Do you dream of being artistic, but do not know where to start?
- Are you ready for a career change?
- Do you want to start a new business, but feel you lack the

creative expertise to make it profitable?
- Do you want to make better creative decisions in your job or business?
- Are you consumed with guilt for spending time on your creative dreams and not giving enough time to loved ones?
- Does self-doubt keep you from taking risks?
- Are you jealous of other people who are achieving what your heart desires?
- What is holding you back from unlocking your creative power?

This is a book about how you can be highly creative in your life so you can turn your ideas and dreams into reality, and experience the joy and fulfillment that comes from it. If you resonate with this statement, then this book is for you.

We can all make our dreams come true. The way to do that is to unlock our creative power. To unlock our creative power, all we need are the right tools – and those tools you will find in this book. I'm here to tell you that if you can think it, you can create it. Consider Walt Disney, a true master of imagination. Disney started with a dream in his mind -- just a dream.

My Personal Journey

I have been a dreamer all my life. My heart has known its creative desires from as far back as I can recall.

In my youth, I played several musical instruments and took dance lessons. I also sketched brilliant murals on my parents' walls, invented ingenious methods of terrorizing my younger sister, and designed, ahem, experimental costumes for my poor cat.

It was also at a young age when I knew that I wanted to be a writer. It was a secret buried deep in my heart. How could I have known? It all began in elementary school when I read the remarkable life story of Catherine the Great of Russia. While reading about her life I dreamed about how magnificent, exotic and powerful of a woman she was, and I fanaticized about being able to tell that kind of story. And so, the day I finished the last chapter and closed the book, my heart decided to write stories like Catherine the Great when I grew up.

I realize that in elementary school I would never have been able to articulate that I was feeling inspired, but looking back now, that is what happened: I was inspired. And while I never did write my Catherine the Great story, as an adult I *have* embraced my writing talents. I have also followed the desires of my heart and made things happen in my life that I dreamed of. But, I must say it was not always an easy journey.

Along my personal journey I discovered the key to unlocking our creative power, which I would like to pass along to you. That key is in this following story:

I spent my early twenties restless and in constant search of *more*. In fact, my father once referred to me as a *rolling stone* (as in "a rolling stone gathers no moss"). After graduating from university, and a short stint in London, this rolling stone moved to Toronto in pursuit of the dream career. By the time I was in my mid-twenties, I had everything I thought I could possibly want: an exciting job, designer clothes, a luxurious condo, a loving partner, friends, family and exotic travel. Yet, this rolling stone was *still* restless and without joy. Worse, I did not understand *why*.

One evening, I sat at my piano and composed a song to lift my spirits. I suddenly became intrigued with this mysterious ability to create music "out of thin air." Like magic, my fingers knew precisely where to go on the keyboard. A strange feeling overcame me: it was as if *I became one with the music.*

Sitting there, I asked myself questions: What is creativity? Where does it come from? Why are some people more creative than others? And was creativity somehow connected to my state of unhappiness?

So, I began to explore my creativity. I enrolled in film school and began writing fiction. I made other courageous changes, such as saying good-bye to my partner, purchasing a house and getting a dog. I had a great job, I was pursing my creative passions and was excited about my future, but there was *still* something holding me back from feeling fulfilled and successful. I did not know *what*.

Well, I turned my attention inward and began my journey of self-discovery. One weekend I participated in a seminar organized by a unique life coach, author and motivational speaker, Dr. Lise Janelle, who is dedicated to helping people lead vibrant, successful lives. According to Dr. Janelle, the key to having a vibrant, successful life is *self-worth*. It is about opening up the heart and loving oneself, and everything we desire flows from that: loving relationships, joy, prosperity, success, health, and so on.

The *Inward Bound* seminar was life-changing. Dr. Janelle told me point blank the reason I was unhappy, restless and not feeling successful was because *my heart was closed*. It was closed and locked because I did not live with gratitude. Since I was not able to open my heart, I could not hear what it was whispering to me. As a result, my creative power was blocked. And since my creative power was blocked, I could not achieve my goals or creative desires. Because I was not achieving my goals or desires, I doubted myself and stopped believing in my abilities...and so the cycle continued.

Right there and then, I decided I wanted to open my heart so I could experience joy, fulfillment and limitless creative expression. So, I connected with my heart. I asked it questions, such as: what will it take for me to be happy and fulfilled? It began whispering to me. It reminded me of that fateful day I finished reading the life story of Catherine the Great, and how sad I felt to end my romance with the story and close the book -- and how much I wanted to *feel* that inspiring connection with my own heart again.

My heart went from a whisper to a scream, shouting: "Write, Shannon! Write from your heart and inspire others!" And so, I began to trust my whispering heart -- and that is how this book was born.

What does this story have to do with creativity, you might be asking?

Creative mastery and self-love go hand-in-hand.

As I have discovered, the key to unlocking our creative power is *to believe in ourselves*. How? We have to let go of self-doubt, which builds obstacles to our dreams and fulfilling our creative desires. The way to let go of self-doubt is to make the whisper of the heart stronger. We strengthen our whispering hearts *by loving ourselves and living with gratitude*. When we love ourselves and live with gratitude, we believe in our abilities, we become more creative, and we are courageous enough to dream and take action steps toward fulfilling that dream. And this is the prominent message of this book.

The Whispering Heart

The reason I called this book *The Whispering Heart: Your Inner Guide to Creativity* is because the heart knows all about our creative dreams, whatever we wish or desire to bring into this world throughout our lifetime, and if we listen to its wisdom, it steers us in the right direction. That direction is toward our purpose in life. Says Marianne Williamson, "The purpose of our lives is to give birth to the best which is within us."

Your life's purpose is what fulfills you and gives you joy and meaning every day, whether it is being an artist, a parent, healer, writer, gardener, or living a life filled with love, gratitude and self-expression. Just as my heart guided me toward my purpose in life, to write and inspire others, your heart will guide you as well. Your heart is your voice of wisdom. When you follow the whispers of your heart you will find creative expression, joy, meaning, fulfillment and success. And for that you cannot go wrong.

> • *Please take some time to sit quietly and connect with your heart: your voice of wisdom. What is it whispering to you? What are its desires? What does it dream of? Grab a notebook and write a few pages (at least three) about whatever your heart is whispering. Do not judge it or question what it tells you. Just write it all down. Take as long as you need to. Once you are finished, please come back and join me, as we will revisit this at a later time.*

How to Use This Book

Throughout this book are a variety of tools, tips and practical exercises to help you unlock your creative power so that you can turn your dreams, whatever they may be, into something real under the sun. I recommend you do these exercises while working your way through the book, or come back to them at a later time if you wish.

Also, throughout the book I draw from my own personal experiences and journey. These background stories or examples are woven throughout -- not because I enjoy talking about myself, but because I feel that by sharing what I have experienced and learned, the good and the bad, it will move or inspire you to make things happen in your own life.

May the wisdom of your whispering heart be your guide.

The Art & Science of Creativity

*The creation of something new is not accomplished by the intellect but
by the play instinct acting from inner necessity.
The creative mind plays with the objects it loves.*
-- Carl Jung

Create *(kre.at') v.t.: To cause to come into existence; originate.*

What is Creativity (and what is it not)?

Each one of us has the power to create. Our creative power comes
from within us: the heart, soul and mind working in harmony. There
inside, our creative power grows with desire until we drum up enough
courage to unleash that creative energy and manifest what the heart
yearns. Until given the green light, our creative energy stays put in a
state of laziness, agitation, bashfulness or excitement.

I say...green light! Get going! Unleash your creative energy and
create anything, and everything, you desire. Do something productive
with your creative energy and turn it into an experience of sheer bliss.
But before you launch into the land of imagination, you may find it
beneficial to get a general overview of creativity.

Simply put, **creativity** is:

> *The power or ability to bring an idea or concept into reality and
> make something new under the sun. It begins with its roots in
> imagination.*

You were born creative and for the remainder of your life you will
continue to exist in this Universe as an energy being in constant motion,
full of dreamy ideas and doing what comes naturally: being creative.

To be creative is to be all that we can humanly be. *To be creative is to
totally express ourselves.* Arguably, that is our ultimate purpose in life:
to totally express ourselves, whether it is a natural expression of love,

joy, gratitude, talent, skill, art, dance, work, sports or gardening.

What creativity is *not* is some weirdness that artists are cursed with as if it was leprosy or a contagious disease. Creativity is not *only* the act of painting on canvas, or directing a film, or drawing cartoons, or dance, or any other career in the arts.

What many people do not seem to realize is that creativity is *problem-solving*, such as coming up with business solutions or new ways of doing things around the house. It is *conceptualizing ideas and plans*, such as furniture design, architecture and marketing communication programs. Creativity is *managing relationships*, like business partnerships and personal relationships; and *deciding what emotions to use* in particular circumstances, like knowing the right time to send your spouse to the doghouse!

Every decision we make uses our creativity.

Having a baby is creation. Raising a family uses creativity. Cooking dinner for your family or friends is also a creative act. So is developing a business plan. Having a dream of something you want to do in your life and making it happen uses your creativity.

One of the greatest myths about creativity is that there is a creative personality, or some unique personality quirks or traits that are a requirement for being creative. I hear this remark all the time: She's the *creative type*. Many people who do not consider themselves *artsy* sadly believe they are not creative. Baloney. Creativity is *not* tied to a particular personality type. We are *all* creative.

Another myth about creativity is the belief that creativity is tied to a high IQ score. This is when a little reframing about intelligence is in order.

According to Harvard psychologist Dr. Howard Gardner, author of *Frames of Mind* (and later made popular by Thomas Armstrong's book *Seven Kinds of Smart)*, we have not one -- but seven -- areas of intelligence. This notion of *multiple intelligences* is at the heart of the field of creativity, and it includes:

1. **Linguistic-Verbal** – *to manipulate words (oral or written).*

2. **Mathematical-Logical** – *to manipulate number systems and logical concepts.*

3. **Spatial** – *to see and manipulate patterns and designs.*

4. **Musical** – *to understand and manipulate musical concepts (tone, rhythm, harmony).*

5. **Bodily-Kinesthetic** – *to use one's body and movement (dance or sports).*

6. **Intrapersonal** – *to understand one's feelings, and to be reflective and philosophical.*

7. **Interpersonal** – *to understand other people's feelings and thoughts.*

Each one of us has a preference or dominance in one or two areas, but we can access all or a combination of intelligence areas throughout our lifetime. When we realize our creativity is not tied to a high IQ score, we can relax…and explore and expand our creative interests.

Where Ideas Come From

Have you ever wondered where ideas come from? Forming an idea is a process like "connecting the dots."

It seems to work like this: an *original idea* starts as a baby thought that bubbles up from nowhere, which makes connections and associations with unrelated thoughts – and it blends and grows like crazy. Next thing you know, you are looking at things in a different way. Happenstance or twist of fate. Just the meandering mind making one brilliant connection after the other and developing something new.

It is the creative process in action.

You could be working in a laundry and the next thing you know you start thinking about "adolescent girls being cruel." What follows is a separate thought about "telekinesis." You connect the two thoughts and – voila – you end up with a famous horror story that shocks people around the world for years to come. This is how Stephen King describes the origins of *Carrie*.

In a way, creativity starts as pure energy because *the ideas that make up your creative thinking are nothing more than electrical impulses in your brain* (powered by the energy of your brainwaves). For the purpose of this book though, it is not where our ideas come from that is most important here: it is what you *do with them* that counts.

Symbolic Thinking

Science tells us that when we are thinking and communicating through "abstract symbols," we are engaging in *symbolic thinking*. Symbolic thinking is the foundation of art, music, language, mathematics and science.

What is most intriguing about symbolic thinking is its origins, which is a contentious issue for anthropologists and archeologists who continually debate *when*, *how* and *why* symbolic thinking was developed in humans. One might assume symbolic thinking first developed when humans became bipedal, discovered fire, or invented tools or weapons. You may recall the powerful images at the beginning of Stanley Kubrick's classic film *2001: A Space Odyssey*.

According to scientists, some 50,000 years ago, in Africa, a "creative explosion" occurred in our evolution when *Homo sapiens*, our first human ancestors, quite suddenly developed new skills and forms of self-expression. They began painting, created music and designed musical instruments. They made decorative jewelry from ostrich eggshells, fashioned clothing and invented advanced tools such as fishing poles and tackle, and bows and arrows. These early ancestors built permanent lodging and used ceremony and ritual to bury the deceased (the origins of the funeral).

This "dawn of culture," when humans began to display abstract thinking and develop culture and art, is widely understood to be the first and most significant cultural event in human history. And here you thought it was Woodstock!

To put it into perspective, our human ancestors (*Homo sapiens*) had been around for approximately *five to seven million years*. Before the dawn, human anatomy and behavioural changes occurred together, and very, very, slowly. Suddenly, the race was on and behavioural changes took the speedway, leaving the human anatomy in the dust. And *modern behaviour*, the way we think abstractly and create today, began to flourish. It all happened in what is referred to as a "blink of an eye" in evolutionary terms.

According to American anthropologist Dr. Richard Klein, author of *The Dawn of Human Culture*, the reason for what he calls this sudden "big bang" of human culture, or consciousness, was a genetic change leading to a fully developed modern brain in our ancestors, which facilitated the capacity for symbolic thinking and language. Shortly thereafter, beginning around 40,000 years ago, there was an expansion of behavioural change that took place across Africa.

While the dawn of culture is a truly significant time in our history, scientists are now finding evidence that humans may have been wearing jewelry, generally understood to be one of the earliest signs of symbolic thinking, as early as 75,000 years ago.

Other scientific theories about this creative explosion include a change in environmental and/or social circumstances driving one thing: survival. It depends on whom you ask, like anything else in science.

Scientists may never have all the answers. One thing is certain: if you thought you do not have a creative bone in your body, think again. Creative thinking is in your genetic make-up, thanks to your early ancestors who experienced the "big bang of human culture, or consciousness."

The future belongs to ideas people.

**Less than 1 per cent of our brainpower is used.
Imagine...**

Give This a Whirl:

Looking at the seven areas of intelligence, which ones do you have a preference for? Which ones are you strong in? Experiment with the different areas over the course of a week (one each day). Try different ways to improve an area that you feel you are not strong in.

The Creative Process is a Journey

If you have to ask what jazz is, you'll never know.
-- Louis Armstrong

The heart whispers to us. The wisdom of the whispering guides us and it comes from our inner selves. This is the place where our dreams begin, whether it is the desire to make a new product, a concept for starting a business, writing a screenplay or novel, drawing, or simply living a way of life that enables us to fully express ourselves creatively.

Sometimes we are not clear on what our creative dreams are. Or we may have too many of them and don't know what feels right or how we could possibly juggle them all. Or we do not know where to start. Or we become clouded with too much noise in the brain and freeze in our tracks, overwhelmed. How do you know what is right for your heart to pursue?

You have likely had an idea that has teased your mind for a while, perhaps several years. It may be something you have wanted to try, or to produce, or experience, and your heart yearns for it. Your heart knows with certainty this is what you want to experience or bring into the world; the same way I knew I wanted to be a writer. Whenever you think about the idea you resonate with it. It is like striking a note on the piano and being in perfect tune with it. It is a "knowing."

However, maybe something has been holding you back from pursuing your dream. If this occurs, the idea begins to gnaw at your guts, scraping away. If you have not taken action to make it happen, such as taking a course or doing your research, you begin to feel annoyed or miffed with yourself. Your heart constantly yearns for it. Your heart aches if you do not do something – *anything*! You may even become seriously depressed if you do not fulfill your creative desires.

For creative geniuses, those who have *mastered their creative desires*, this whispering of their guiding hearts completely takes over their lives. They get a gem of an idea and become infatuated with it, even obsessed, and then work madly on their projects around the clock. When creative geniuses are in the proverbial creative state of *flow*, nothing stops them. Getting in their way is like standing between a wild hungry dog and

24

a piece of juicy red meat. Creative geniuses can easily disappear off the face of the planet and reappear only to get a breath of fresh air, garnering little notice from anyone.

Canadian singer/songwriter Neil Young is one of those creative geniuses. After reading Young's biography, I was inspired by his unrelenting, insatiable creative drive, which has resulted in a prolific artist who has tremendous commercial success. Love him or not, he is a true creative genius who constantly reinvents himself, tries new things and masters his creative desires. He is also renowned for his disappearing acts and reappearing with reams of new creative work.

Madonna is another example of a true creative genius. As a multi-dimensional artist, she follows her heart and constantly reinvents herself to be relevant to today's audiences. I must admit that early in her career I did not connect with her. Today, as a grown woman I have genuine respect for Madonna. She follows the whisper of her heart and has an insatiable drive to continue to be all she can be creatively: a mother, an author of children's books, singer, songwriter, actor and the ultimate stage performer. Again, love her, or not, she is an inspiring, commendable, creative genius who listens to the wisdom of her heart.

To be all that we can be creatively, to be a creative genius in our own way, we need to understand that creativity is a *process*, and to have the ability to recognize this creative process for what it is.

Processing the Creative Journey

The creative process is truly a journey. It is like getting in your car without a map, pointing the vehicle in a direction, putting the peddle to the metal and then taking turns at random. The purpose is to reach a desired destination, yet you enjoy the unfamiliar scenery along the way. There are a few points about this journey -- the creative process -- that are valuable to understand. It is not a scientific explanation about the creative process, rather what I personally believe is important to comprehend for the purposes of creative achievement.

First, creativity begins with *inspiration*. Ping! An idea is born. You get excited. Your heart goes from a whisper to a scream, shouting, "Get that damn idea in motion!" It is a *eureka* moment. More than likely you have this ongoing chat with yourself....I can do it...no I can't...I want to do it....I would love to do it...but I can't...yes, yes, yes... This chatting may have sticking power and, if so, you follow the idea with full force. Or the idea may wane for a while and show up when you least expect it; like when you are shopping at the supermarket or waking you in the night.

What is inspiration? Inspiration is pretty cool to experience, but is tricky to define or articulate. It is like trying to describe spirit, love or joy. Inspiration comes from our core essence. One thing is certain: you know what inspiration feels like when you are experiencing it. To me, inspiration feels like a *surge of positive energy blended with clarity of vision and desire.* Inspiration takes on a life force of its own, taking charge and leading the way. Interestingly enough, the root of the word *inspire* is "to breathe into."

Second, you must be aware that an idea is simply the beginning of a journey you are about to embark on; you will need to take action to take it to the next level. The creative process has a beginning, middle and end. What is important is to not focus so much on racing to the end to achieve results, but to just start the process by taking *action steps.* The journey starts by taking that first step, then another; one step right in front of the other toward a desired destination. Maybe at the beginning they are baby steps, but soon you could be taking giant leaps.

Thirdly, after you are inspired, and are fully aware that you need to take action, *analytical thinking* kicks in. You think about it from every angle. You do your homework. You gain perspective. It is at this point that analytical thinking is beneficial when it comes to creativity. You ask yourself smart, reasonable questions such as: Is this a good idea? How will it fare in the marketplace? Is it commercial enough? Can I make a living? Is it original? How can I make this idea big? How far will it take me? Will it make me rich? Who would be interested? Who the heck cares anyway?

Developing a strategic plan to map out your vision is wise, but be aware that it may take a long time for your idea to come to fruition, possibly years. When a mother gives birth, she expects that one day her child will be old enough that she can carry a conversation with him/her. However, first the baby needs to babble, then crawl, walk, learn to speak, and so on. It is the same for the creative journey. *Your "baby" can take years! So if you develop a strategic plan, you may want to be projecting years ahead.* Just do not throw the baby out with the bathwater.

We may become frustrated when our ideas do not come to fruition as quickly as we wish. It can be like watching a pot of water on a stove start to boil. It may even feel like torture. Conversely, our ideas may take off faster than our wildest imagining thought possible. Regardless, it is best to enjoy the journey because we learn a lot about life and ourselves along the way. Let the ego slip away and stay in touch with your heart. In other words, buckle up and enjoy the ride!

Fourthly, *passion* -- the gasoline of life – fuels creativity. Passion is an experience of joy. It unfolds possibilities. By now you have toyed with the idea, maybe in fits and spurts over time, but regardless of what curve balls may be thrown your way the passion for your idea remains constant, like a computer software program running in the background that keeps your system going. Passion is the gasoline of life; it is such a powerful force that it propels us toward achieving our goals. It never fails to fuel your creative drive.

Fifthly, part of this process may be to *transcend self-doubt thoughts,* such as: "I do not have the ability to achieve this." You look for support, validation and ways to boost your confidence to help get you through to the next level.

Lastly, at some point you either become *committed* to your idea or dream -- or *you let it go* into the graveyard of ideas in the sky. By this stage, you have played with your idea and passion has consumed you. If obstacles arise that seem insurmountable, such as the fear of running out of money, how are you certain that you are whole-heartedly committed? Well, you go hog-wild to see your dream to the end. Like Superman or Wonder Woman, you leap over those hurdles! Crush those obstacles! This is when you know you are committed to fulfilling your creative desires. If not, another idea bites the dust. And that is okay.

Know that there is benefit to making a commitment to yourself. When we make commitments to ourselves, things seem to almost magically happen far more quickly than when we wobble with uncertainty or are unclear -- or uncommitted.

The Creative Journey

- *An idea is born out of inspiration.*

- *You become aware that action steps need to be taken.*

- *You analyze the idea.*

- *Passion, the gasoline of life, fuels the idea.*

- *You may need to transcend self-doubt thoughts.*

- *You make a whole-hearted commitment, or let the idea go to the graveyard of ideas.*

Give These a Whirl:

1. *Please revisit what you wrote earlier about what your heart whispers to you; the first exercise we did early in the introduction. What are your heart's desires? What is the big idea? What is your creative dream? When you are ready, make a commitment to yourself to see your creative dream through to the end. If you find you are not sure or ready to make a commitment, know it is okay. Do it when you are ready.*
   Feel free to use this copy as a template or basis to write your own:

   I, (your name), am whole-heartedly committed to my idea (insert your idea) and/or fulfilling my creative dream (insert your dream). I am ready, willing and able to take action steps enabling me to get me where I want to go. I now take the first step toward manifesting my creative dream.

2. *The next time you are inspired about anything at all, whether it is an idea, a change you want to make in your life or something new to try out, take a moment to explore what that*

inspiration feels like. Embrace it. Capture the moment in writing (in a notebook or journal) so you can refer to it at a later time.

Why Dreams Get Quashed Before They Begin

*What lies behind us and what lies before us are tiny matters
compared to what lies within is.
-- Ralph Waldo Emerson*

You have probably wondered at some point in your life why some people are more creative than others. Or why some people are able to make their dreams happen and others are not as fortunate. Or what makes a creative genius a creative genius.

Well, we know that creative ability is not necessary tied to a high IQ score. *A creative genius is a person who masters their creative desires.* As Thomas Edison, one of history's most famous creative geniuses, once remarked, "Genius is one percent inspiration and ninety-nine percent perspiration."

A creative genius is someone who can *dream up an idea and take action steps to make it a reality.*

While I am certain everyone has his or her individual opinions, and there certainly may be several contributing factors, the reason some people are more highly creative than others is largely based on how we, in general, are *socialized.*

Most of us are born with pure, raw, creative intelligence. As children we are innately curious and highly imaginative. Children ask a zillion questions, and are constantly seeking truth, knowledge and guidance. How often do you hear...Why? How? When? Where?

When children are engaging in this kind of thinking and questioning, they are using the problem-solving hemisphere of their brains -- their creative side. However, experts say at an early age (usually when they begin school, according to studies) most children lose the ability to be creative geniuses. Why? It is at this point that they begin to *conform.* They follow society's rules. Sadly, it is also at this stage that creativity ceases to be nurtured.

I remember my kindergarten teacher insisting I print with my right hand rather than my left hand, which I was happily using. As scientists now know, the left hand is connected to the right brain, which is the creative side of the brain; and right hand is connected to the left brain, the analytical side. The brain is like any other muscle; when flexed and used it becomes stronger. By using the left hand, it strengthens the right hemisphere, therefore strengthening the creative side of the brain. By switching hands from left to right, my creative side was not exercised as it would have been had my teacher not made me switch. While I do not believe this is common practice with teachers today, why did my teacher do that? So my printing resembled everyone else's: to conform.

As a society, it would be a good investment for us to pay closer attention to *what* and *how* we teach our children in preparation to be fully actualized creative beings. It has been my experience that the way we teach not only children, but also adults in university and college, is too "do as I tell you" authoritarian, especially as far as the creative spirit is concerned. Unfortunately, teachers themselves are no longer creative... and so what happens? They are teaching children to conform.

Children, in particular, are often not encouraged to question the teacher's knowledge or the rules, but are expected to accept what the teacher, the authority figure, dictates. Think back to when you were in school. Does this sound familiar? Most teachers do not like to be questioned or challenged. It makes them feel insecure. I know; I am a teacher. This does little to develop independent, creative thinking and expression in our people, and is not the best investment in our society.

When I first began teaching a public relations course at a university, I decided to incorporate my personal philosophy about creativity into a teaching style more conducive to creative thinking, one not overly authoritarian. I really let my students "question." My style was unconventional, which was difficult for some students because they are accustomed to having rigid boundaries drawn for them, and being told what to do. I discovered that students with open minds and the desire for creative expression were far more open to my style and, as a result, did exceptionally well in my class. Not only did they do well, they developed a hunger to learn more about themselves and their creative nature. Those students who followed their hearts gave me enormous inspiration.

Human beings are socialized to *not* question or defy authority figures, rather we are socialized to *conform* (all for one and one for all) and *think analytically*. These are society's values. We are encouraged to concentrate our studies on mathematics, science and language, and leave the arts to extracurricular activities. We are encouraged to accept things the way they are. There are always exceptions to the rule obviously, but as far as our education system is concerned we do a fabulous job of preparing our youngsters for careers in science and technology, medicine, finance, law and the military, but do little to encourage them to have fertile creative minds and to be fully developed creative beings.

Keep in mind the whispers of the heart that guides us through life often develop early in childhood. What do you think happens to that inner guide when children start to conform? Yep, it gets quashed. Squished like a bug on a windshield.

Adam dreamed of being an artist when he was a child. It was in his youth when the whisper of his heart spoke to him. When it was time for him to choose his vocation, he expressed his desire to go to art school. Unfortunately, his family did not agree with his choice because they feared it meant a dismal future (how would he ever pay the bills?), and instead directed him to the field of science and technology where he would be sure to find work. Adam abided by his parents wishes, tossing aside his art, therefore tossing aside his creative spirit. As an adult, at the core of his inner self is a creative genius bubbling away, but that bubbling spirit has been turned down a notch to simmer because he was led to conform to a way of life that is more acceptable by society.

This may or may not pertain to you, but if you have children in school I encourage you to take a moment to think about *what* they are learning and the *way* they are learning as it relates to their imagination and creative development. Our children are the future leaders of our society, therefore it would be a good investment if, together, we all played a role in helping them become independent, creative thinkers and learn to express their creative spirits.

It was at an early age when I knew I wanted to be a writer. It was a secret buried in my heart, yet not one teacher encouraged me to listen to it, to let it unfold. It was not until later in adulthood when that whispering became so strong it begged and shouted at me to take action, letting it come to fruition. The whispering was always there as my guide, but sadly ignored.

A creative genius is a person who masters their creative desires.

Questions to Ask Yourself:

What motivates you? What stimulates your passion and drive? Be honest with what is rolling around in your head, because your whispering heart will know if you are not. It is the best lie detector ever built.

Try This:

To strengthen the creative right side of your brain, try this exercise. For an entire day, use your left hand for doing all your daily activities, such as brushing your teeth, writing, opening doors, picking up objects and using the mouse on your computer (this is especially good). If you are naturally left-handed, do the reverse and strengthen the analytical side of your brain.

When the Creative Charge Goes...Kaput!

Whenever I choose between two evils,
I always like the one I haven't tried before.
-- Mae West

Ping! You have an idea. You are on a roll in this excitable state of charged creative energy. You plug away at it, time goes by and suddenly...*wham*! You hit a wall. Your creative charge goes...kaput. You get a flat.

Creative energy is like electricity. In its natural state it flows effortlessly and abundantly. But if the plug is pulled on your creative power, it means you have run into an *obstacle*.

What is an obstacle?

There are a number of different emotions that prevent us from connecting with the heart that knows and nurtures our creative desires, and steers us in the right direction in life. These emotions are obstacles that block our creative charge and hold us back from reaching our dreams. Some obstacles may be fleeting, while others are more aggressive, to the point of debilitation.

Ultimately, if we are not connecting with the heart, the biggest enemy of creativity creeps in and makes itself right at home -- **self-doubt**. Self-doubt ruthlessly quashes, or at the extreme, totally obliterates creativity. Self-doubt becomes a force of its own. Self-doubt has no sensitive feelings, no dreams of its own, no remorse, but is a cold and hard killing force with one purpose in mind: death of one's spirit. Self-doubt is the serial killer of creativity. Not only will it kill your own creativity, it will seek the death of others. Its poisonous venom knows no boundaries. Okay, okay, so I'm being a bit melodramatic, but I can't emphasize enough that self-doubt is a huge obstacle for the creative mind.

Here are some examples of other obstacles that prevent us from experiencing our creative power and therefore reaching our dreams or goals. By gaining perspective, we can remove these obstacles.

FEAR

Fear is nasty for creative people because it stifles creativity, preventing us from achieving our dreams. Fear takes over our thoughts and bodies, and immobilizes us. Fear happens when we "go into the future" and focus on what may or may not happen, rather than being "fully engaged in the moment" where creativity occurs.

Fear can appear in many forms: Fear of failure. Fear of success. Fear of making mistakes. Fear of criticism. Fear of inability or lack of talent. Fear of losing a friend or loved one if we follow our heart. Fear of the unknown. Fear of change. Fear of being stuck. Fear of making a decision. Fear of poverty.

Each one of us has the ability to overcome our fears, though what works for one person may not necessarily work for the other. What is important is to identify the fear and strive to overcome it. Following is a sample of some of those fears we often share as it relates to creativity, put into perspective.

Fear of Failure:

Failure is an illusion. No matter what the outcome is, as long as you are driven by your passion and take action steps toward making your dream come true, you cannot lose. There is much to gain. Do not let the fear of failure stand in the way of your dream. Perhaps by trying something new you are augmenting skills, developing a budding talent, or broadening your mind, tastes and experiences. Is this failure? I don't think so. You have truly achieved something, even if it is not exactly what you had intended.

If you do not reach your goals, or if your project is not going exactly the way you envisioned, take a closer look at what you *have* accomplished -- and learn from it. Apply what you have learned and you gain valuable perspective.

If you ask people what motivates them to be successful, often they claim the fear of failure (in one way or another) keeps them marching on...or flying by the seat of their pants. This is the value of having a fear of failure: it pushes us forward. However, scaring the bejeezus out of oneself is not the most productive or healthy means to motivate us.

35

My young actor friend, Nathan, has a great perspective when it comes to fear of failure. As a 15 year-old, he has much wisdom to offer any adult. He goes into his auditions believing in himself and the possibility of failure does not seem to enter his mind. He always leaves his auditions feeling good about the overall experience. When someone once asked him if, as an actor, he had a fear of rejection (failure), he declared the fear of rejection was silly because "it was nothing personal." Words of wisdom from a young lad.

Fear of Success:

Ahh…this is one that is not always obvious, or certainly not one we like to admit. What if I become -- *heaven forbid* -- successful? What if my manuscript is – *gulp* -- published? What if the critics like it? What if my painting is – *eek* – sold? What if my new gadget design makes it to market and is sold internationally? It is a matter of self-worth; to have the confidence to believe in ourselves and feel we are worthy of success. It is important to feel we are worthy of receiving what we desire from the world. It is also important to feel we are worthy of donating our genius to the world. We all deserve joy, fulfillment and success.

One evening I was having a lovely dinner with a friend who, at the time, was an emerging film and television producer. When I asked him about his latest project, he became silent, edgy and squirmed in his seat, to the point of making me uncomfortable. Being presumptuous, I asked him if business was okay, which he replied, "Yeah, that's the problem!" As it turned out, his company was rapidly taking off and it scared the heck out of him. He admitted his biggest fear was making it "big." When I asked him what would be the worst possible thing that could happen by being successful, and the best possible outcome, he relaxed. Weeks after our dinner, he told me that he kept revisiting our conversation and worked on changing his perspective. Today, he has a flourishing film and television production company.

Once we reach success, or are on the way there, we can also experience the fear of losing our friends who are not feeling successful themselves. Rather than being worried that you will lose your friends, encourage them to follow their hearts so they, too, can be successful. Become a source of inspiration for them. As well, you will find new friends that will inspire you and encourage you to continue along your path.

Fear of Making Mistakes:

Yikes! The fear of *all* fears. First of all, there is no such thing as mistakes – only lessons. When we are grateful for the people in our lives and for the events that happen to us, good and bad, we see "the gift." The gifts (benefits) we get from our lessons are invaluable, so never dismiss or diminish their impact. As Albert Einstein once said, "In the middle of difficulty lies opportunity."

Take the view that any mistake you make is a valuable lesson and you free yourself of the shackles that chain your creative freedom. So, go ahead and make lots of valuable lessons. Just be sure to learn from them. Not only will you become more creative, you gain wisdom.

Because the fear of making a mistake is such a huge obstacle that holds people back from pursuing their creative interests, we explore this topic in more detail later in the book.

Fear of Criticism:

Many highly creative people, especially artists, are plagued with fragile egos. They take criticism to heart, which leads to discouragement and feelings of self-doubt and inadequacy. Remember this: ego kills creativity. Let ego slip away and *create from the heart*. When it comes to criticism, no one can beat us up more than ourselves and no one can knock us down more than ourselves. However, *constructive criticism* is good -- we grow! If we feel someone is judging us though, it is because we are judging a part of ourselves.

We have a need as a society to be accepted and loved. However, what is most important is that we accept and love ourselves. What anyone else thinks about you or your creative work or dream is their issue: it is a mere reflection of their own inner world, positive or negative, and they are projecting their inner world onto you. Their issue has nothing to do with you. It is advisable to adopt this way of thinking: "What other people think is none of my business." Do not take criticism to heart. Learn from it, apply it and move on.

After I wrote the first draft of my first screenplay, I decided to "sit on it" until I determined my next steps. Rather than sending it to producers to review and possibly agree to produce it, I continued tinkering with the copy to make it better; at least that was how I justified my "procrastination" (fear) of not sending it out. I was fearful of hearing it belonged in the category of one-notch-below-garbage. The script sat on my desk for ages before I finally jailed my ego and drummed up the courage to send a copy to a producer.

Eventually, I got my criticism, but not in the terrible way my mind imagined it would be. What I got instead was valuable constructive feedback that encouraged me to write a second draft, which was remarkably better than the first.

Fear of Inability:

When it comes to creativity, the fear of inability is usually translated into a fear of lack of talent. There are so many people that I know who express interest in developing a new skill, or hobby, or switching careers, but lack the confidence to try it because they fear they will not be good at it. They fear stepping outside their zone of comfort. Talent is not necessarily vital to being creative. In some respects talent is irrelevant. What is important is to learn the necessary skills or brush up on your knowledge, and take action steps toward what you desire.

Go for it! Do not focus your energy on whether you have talent or not. Dive into your desires. If it satisfies your whispering heart, that is what matters. Besides, you never know if you have talent or ability unless you give it a whirl, and you may be pleasantly surprised with your discovery. Remind yourself there is nothing you cannot accomplish. By taking action toward what you desire you increase your self-worth and become more confident and creative.

When Sarah, an acquaintance, left her job as a communication advisor in a high-profile company to start her own consulting business, a dream she had for many years, she had this niggling fear that she lacked the ability to succeed as a businesswoman. She had many years of experience as a communication professional, and certainly the talent to succeed, but lacked the confidence in her ability as a sole proprietor.

She was afraid of not landing new business and not being able to pay her bills. She was afraid of putting her neck on the line and not making sound recommendations to clients, because as an independent consultant she no longer had a large company standing behind her where she could hide if she made a "mistake."

Step by step, she did what was necessary to get it going so she could survive. She had always known the value of networking, so she networked to find new business. She created a business model that worked best for her. She developed confidence over time to put herself on the line and learned the skills necessary to survive as an independent consultant. Today, her communication consulting company has grown well beyond her expectations.

Fear of the Unknown:

Fear of the unknown is closely linked to fear of making a mistake or failure. This is when we focus on the uncertainty of what lies on the road ahead and become afraid of negative outcomes. When this sets in, we question the decisions we make, or our abilities, or how important a dream or goal is to us. It can cause us to stay in our comfort zone rather than venturing into the great unknown toward our dream.

For instance, Cathy dreamed of moving to Paris to begin writing a novel based on a true story that took place there, but the fear of not being able to find a job, or not being able to find a place to live, or not being able to make new friends – all factors of the unknown -- held her back from experiencing that dream. She focused on negative possibilities, rather than on possible *good* experiences and opportunities that could come out of it.

To face the fear of the known, we must be willing to walk into it. The best way to do this is to ask ourselves what is the worst thing that could happen and what would be the best possible outcome, and realize that everything in between is a growing experience. When we get the bigger picture, we can take the steps forward toward what we desire.

Fear of Poverty:

When we focus on money not coming our way, strangely enough

39

it really does not come to us. When we focus on the bank account depleting, strangely enough it continues depleting even more. When we are so worried that by living our dreams we will not be able to pay the bills and, as a result, will eventually land in the poorhouse, we get so caught up in that worry energy that we get paralyzed and cannot go forward.

A friend of mine, a lawyer, was out of work for more than a year after a series of unfortunate and uncontrollable incidents. Not only is he a good lawyer, he is also a brilliant artist who sketches the human form like no one else I know. During the time he was unemployed, he was so worried about his bank account depleting, and becoming impoverished, that he could not shift his mental energy to do what would have been good for his spirit: his art. He was blocked. And because his spirit was blocked, his energy was held back from attracting his dream job. Finally, one day he picked up his art again and, shortly thereafter, he landed his dream job…with money in the bank.

Rather than being fearful of having no money or becoming poor, set your sights on having prosperity – and take action steps in that direction. It is merely a slight shift in thinking with an emphasis on the positive. And always keep your focus on your goal.

GUILT

Guilt is equally nasty for the creative person and it is essentially a wheel-spinning emotion that wastes a lot of energy. When we feel guilty, we feel as though we have done something wrong or failed at an obligation to someone. We are stuck in the past because of something we did or did not do. And so, we can't move forward.

We may experience guilt for taking too much time for ourselves or for our creative work. Guilt for not making enough time for loved ones. Guilt for making big changes that impact other people. Guilt for saying *no* -- or *yes*. Guilt for spending money on our creative projects. Guilt for being successful.

Guilt is an emotion that holds us back from being creative. These are some typical situations where we often feel guilty when it comes to creativity.

Guilt for Not Spending Time with Loved Ones:

Sometimes our loved ones make us feel guilty for not spending enough time with them. Your child may one day ask you why you never spend time with them anymore. Or you may feel guilty because your pet needs more attention or exercise. Or perhaps a partner feels you are too absorbed in your work and not putting enough effort into the relationship. The feeling of guilt enters like an unwanted intruder whenever you turn your attention to your dream. This is not healthy for creativity and you would be well served to change your perspective.

To a point, it is okay to be selfish with how you spend your time and energy. When you realize how important your creative dream is to you, especially when aligned with your heart, life becomes more enriched and joyful, and you therefore have more to offer loved ones. Stop feeling guilty. Share your feelings with the person who is the source of your guilt, and help them understand that you are following your heart and it also helps them and ultimately your relationship.

If the issue is a pet, come up with alternatives. My dog Harry demands a lot of attention. I began feeling guilty for spending time on my creative projects and not giving him the attention he deserves. So, I hired a dog walker. It has turned out to be a good solution for a number of reasons: for a small price I have opened up my time more, Harry gets his exercise and his terrific dog walker earns a living.

Keep in mind how you spend your time is an investment in YOU.

Guilt for Spending Money:

Creativity can come attached with hard costs, such as a fee for a course, books, movies, art supplies, equipment or other materials. Perhaps we are required to travel, or rent an office or studio, or change our lifestyle. If we see our bank account depleting and then worry (fear) about how we will pay the bills, we may begin to feel guilty for spending money on our creative endeavours. A loved one such as a parent or spouse can also, with the best of intentions, make us feel guilty for spending our money.

When this happens, our dream may become less meaningful to us, to the point we shelve it or abandon it completely. If this sounds familiar, it is important to change your perspective.

If you ever feel guilty about spending money on your creative endeavours, project yourself in the future and visualize what life would be like if you actually completed what you set out to achieve. Would it give you joy? Make you feel fulfilled? Enriched? How far could your wings take you? Spending money on what broadens you as a creative person also benefits others around you, enriching your relationships. The money you spend on your dream is an important, and often necessary, investment in your creativity and happiness. How much is joy worth to you? There is a lot of value when we take this perspective.

Guilt for Making a Change:

When we decide to follow our dreams, we may need to make changes in work or lifestyle; some may be subtle, others more dramatic. These decisions can be difficult for us, or loved ones, leading to feelings of guilt. For instance, we may have to switch jobs, sell assets, travel extensively or relocate to another country, which may be especially trying if you have a family to support.

When I was in my restless early twenties, I decided a radical lifestyle change was in order. I packed a bag, said goodbye to my boyfriend, friends and family, and hopped on a plane bound for Europe. I felt terribly guilty for leaving my boyfriend behind because I was concerned he would be lonely without me. One night, I called my boyfriend who, wiggly as a worm, told me he had found someone else. Obviously he was not lonely! After an hour of tears, I no longer felt guilty for my decision and I began embracing the change I made. I now realize that change was the best experience for me, because it was the impetus that led me to follow my dream.

If you find yourself feeling guilty because of a change you made, or plan to make, understand that by following your heart it is good for you and for your family members. Identify all the benefits that will come from the situation and you will relieve yourself of guilty feelings.

Guilt for Being Successful:

Have you ever been in a situation where you were riding high on an achievement and someone close to you knocked the wind out of your sails? They left you feeling guilty for your success, to the point you avoided discussing it, downplayed it or even sabotaged it. It is likely they were projecting their own desires and dreams, and possibly failures, onto you. They felt resentful.

When people are resentful of our success, it is a situation that needs to be tenderly managed. If you ever experience this guilt, having a discussion to express your concerns or feelings is invaluable. Together, figure out how you being successful benefits them. Regardless, it is important to not let others deflate you and your achievements, especially loved ones.

I have noticed in some relationships where the female earns more money than her male partner, rather than celebrating her success she downplays it, so the male does not feel jealous or bad about himself. In these cases, the woman is doing herself a grave disservice by deflating her achievement and glory, and making herself "smaller." If you find yourself in this situation, if your financial rewards or success is greater than your mate's (regardless of gender), it is best to communicate feelings and try to reach an understanding. Avoiding this matter does not serve you. Instead, give your mate an opportunity to feel stimulated to grow as well.

RESENTMENT

Resentment is bitterness or annoyance provoked by the perception of unfair treatment, which often appears as *anger* -- to the point of hostility. Resentment is negative energy that only hurts us, and holds us back from being all we can be creatively.

We may resent a colleague for coming up with a hotter idea than ours, or a boss for not giving us a promotion. Or we resent a friend who has criticized our creative work. Or we resent a friend who has achieved something we deeply desire for ourselves. Or we resent a parent for not encouraging us to follow our creative interests, or for not putting us through art college. Or we resent a child for being too needy and derailing our plans. We become a bitter sourpuss.

When we feel resentful of situations or towards people who have done us wrong, we only hurt ourselves. We get angry. We become bitter. Or, we obsess, hold grudges, dig our heels into the ground or act out. Instead of moving forward, we remain in the past. Even when good things happen to others around us, we can feel resentful. When we are resentful, we also stunt our creativity. Here are some of the "biggies" as far as how resentment impacts creativity.

Resentment of Critics:

As any creative knows, people are quick to give their opinions, solicited or unsolicited. If we are feeling insecure about our talent or ability, we can take criticism to heart. I have found that people who feel inadequate about their creative work often were harshly criticized as children (by either adults or peers) and they carried the drama of the incident with them into adulthood, which contributed to their feelings of inadequacy.

By being resentful of others we only hurt ourselves. Instead, it is better to thank people for their opinions/criticism and find the benefit in it. We learn from them and therefore, when you take this perspective, it becomes a positive situation rather than a negative one, which only helps us to be more creative.

When I first began my career at a prestigious firm, a boss continuously criticized my news release writing. No matter how hard I tried, my news releases were never good enough. When he gave me back my drafts with his umpteen edits in red pen, I closed my office door and cried my heart out. I resented him in those moments, as nice a guy as he was. Over time, I began to notice every subsequent news release I wrote became better than the previous one. My writing was rapidly improving and I was gaining self-confidence along the way. It took a while, but I realized he was not criticising my work to be mean, rather he was grooming me to be a high-achieving professional. Today, I have much to thank him for.

Resentment of Past "Bad" Events:

How many times have you looked back at a situation or event that occurred in the past and resented it, perhaps to the point of hatred?

Perhaps you were fired from your job, or had a car accident. When past events are perceived as something "bad," it can be like a ghost that follows us wherever we go.

However, when we strive to see how we benefited from it, we get a bigger picture and find a perspective that is balanced -- and we can appreciate the event or situation. We can use that information to be more creative.

And so, to put it into perspective, let's say getting fired from a job that "was a dead end anyway" helped you land a job far more meaningful or inspiring. At your new job, you just so happened to meet the love of your life. When you look back in time, as you are looking lovingly into the eyes of your mate, you are no longer resentful of that boss who gave you the pink slip.

Or, if you had a car accident, maybe it made you realize how precious life is, which forced you to make changes to follow your heart and write a novel -- your life-long dream. So, when you look back, as you are signing your first autograph at your book launch, you are no longer resentful of the accident itself or the person who rear-ended you.

It is the same for people that we perceive as having treated us badly or unfairly. When we identify what we have learned from the person, and how they have helped us grow, we are better able to let resentment slip away, thank them and open the heart.

Through mind-body work I did over the years, I discovered that, as I child, I was resentful of the birth of my younger brother. It was not about my brother per se, but it was about my parents bringing into the world a boy (after three girls) who got all the attention and, in my childish eyes, took away my glory as a girl – because he was a boy. My resentment manifested itself in a variety of ways on a subconscious level. At the drastic end of the scale, I hated being a girl. I wished to be a boy because I experienced the value society places on a boy: a cherished boy passes on the noble family name to the next generation. When my brother was born, the world said, "Finally, they have a boy!" My young ears heard, "You are girl, therefore you are not worthy."

Subconsciously, this feeling of being "second in value" held me back from achieving my potential as a creative being. Why? As a girl I felt inferior. I had a lack of self-confidence in my abilities. I perceived male qualities as being more powerful than female qualities. However, it also became a catalyst to prove that I was going to be as good if not better than a boy. As I became a young woman, I placed my values in the areas men value in society: career, work, finance. I stuffed my femininity in a closet because I saw it as a "weakness," so I was never truly in touch with my female attributes of intuition, healing, nurturing, family, compassion and creation. Instead, I worked extremely hard at my career, like a man in a man's world, and avoided my sensitive side.

Once I became aware of these deep feelings of resentment that sabotaged me on the subconscious level, I worked hard consciously to overcome them. How? I found gratitude for the birth of my brother and, most importantly, for my feminine qualities. I now see the female attributes of nurturing, compassion, healing and so forth as *strengths*, not weaknesses. There is a lot of power in being a woman. I have since embraced womanhood and as my femininity blossomed, so too has my creativity.

ANGER

Anger is a powerful emotion. We often get angry with ourselves for not achieving our goals. Or we get angry with others for blocking us, and so we play the blame game. Or we can get angry at an unexpected situation that costs us the money we put aside for our dreams.

Anger can be used to motivate us and as catalyst for change. In short bursts, anger can be a healthy way to get our creative power fired up. However, in the longer-term, anger takes us away from the heart and therefore does not serve our best interests creatively. It is good to use the anger initially to give us a creative boost, but it is more ideal to release the anger and strive to find balance in order to create from the heart.

INFATUATION

Infatuation leads to resentment. In other words, resentment is the end result of being infatuated.

When we are infatuated with something or someone, it is not coming from the heart. Sure, initially it feels good to be infatuated and we get a real high from it. Being infatuated with something (an idea) or a person (famous celebrity or mentor) can initially lead to creation (an idea or project). However, when we are infatuated we are elated. We are *only* seeing all the "positives" in a situation or a person and not experiencing a *balanced perspective*. Being infatuated eventually leads to being resentful of the very thing or person you were infatuated with.

For instance, if you "fall in love" with the idea for a project and work your butt off night and day trying to get it off the ground, I guarantee there will come a time when you become resentful of the time it takes away from other areas of your life, and then you resent the project itself. Does this sound familiar? If you are infatuated with a person, such as a mentor, you are only seeing the "positive" traits in them. Since we all have "perceived" positive and negative traits, there will come a time or situation when you are exposed to the "negatives," and you become resentful of them. You go from wanting to be around the person all the time to avoiding their telephone calls.

Whenever we "fall into infatuation" with something or someone, it eventually leads to resentment. It is best to find a balanced state where we see both the positives *and* the negatives or the drawbacks, and do not get elated. When we are elated we eventually do the opposite: crash. What goes up must come down. We become resentful. Feelings of resentment take us away from the heart…and we stop creating.

JEALOUSY

When other people close to us are achieving success, it can be difficult emotionally if we are struggling with our own creativity and not feeling good about ourselves. This can lead to resenting those people because we are *jealous*. Jealousy happens when we are afraid we will not have what our heart desires and we see someone else get what we want. Instead, it is better to be happy for those people we are jealous of and concentrate our energy on what is in our heart.

Years ago, one of my girlfriends began to have amazing career opportunities come her way that I was dreaming of. She was not looking for these opportunities to happen either, they just were. Being a green-eyed monster I teased her about it, but really deep down I was resentful.

I was faced with a choice: be happy for my friend or lose her. Her friendship means a great deal to me and I clearly did not want to lose her. After some thought, I opened my heart to her and began to be happy for the joy she was experiencing, rather than a green-eyed monster. I encouraged her to embrace the opportunities and grow. By doing so, I found it released my negative feelings and I channelled the energy toward my own creativity.

PAIN AND PLEASURE

What if you turned pleasant feelings into creative energy? Pleasure of the heart is good. And there is nothing wrong with pleasing your senses (romance, food, wine), as long as you keep in perspective what is good for your heart (love and joy).

Conversely, what if you harnessed painful emotions you may be experiencing, such as *heartache* or *sadness* and, instead of feeling resentment of whatever is causing you pain, turned the pain into creative energy?

As human beings we are constantly seeking pleasurable experiences and run away from painful experiences. Since nature looks for balance, one thing is certain: there will always be both pleasure *and* pain, just as there will always be light *and* darkness. There will always be experiences that are pleasing to the senses, such as making love, celebrations and joyful friendships. There will always be painful experiences, from death of loved ones, to betrayal, to marriage break-ups. We learn from both pleasure *and* pain, and both experiences help us be more creative.

When harnessed and positively channelled, painful emotions (heartache, sadness) can especially be powerful catalysts for creativity. We can use pain to our creative advantage. When channelled into positive, productive energy, we can transcend resentment of the person or situation that is causing the painful emotion. This is healthy for us.

There is a scene in the movie *Something's Gotta Give*, with Diane Keaton and Jack Nicholson that provides a great example. Keaton's character, a middle-aged, divorced writer falls in love with Nicholson's character, an elderly playboy. Inevitably, she experiences heartache. So what does the character do? She pours all her emotions, love and anger, into writing a play. On one level it is hilarious, but what is interesting is the message it delivers: *turn pain and pleasure into creative energy*.

Paul Simon used the painful emotions of his marriage break-up, along with a dash of humour, to come up with *50 Ways To Leave Your Lover*, a song that hit the top of the charts in 1976. James Hetfield, lead singer of heavy-metal band *Metallica*, also knows about turning pain into creativity. As a teenager (like so many other teens), Hetfield used music as an escape from a bitter home life and formed the band in the '80s. Hetfield's music stemmed from pure anger. That anger made *Metallica* one of the top heavy-metal bands in the world -- selling 100 million albums.

The Mexican artist, Frida Kahlo, lived in pain following a horrific accident that left her with life-long disabilities. She harnessed that pain and, as she said, "painted my own reality," much of it from her bed. Her vibrant and stunning portraits and images of Mexico and all that inspired her are the gifts she gave to the world.

Turn pain and pleasure into creative energy.

Self-Worth

Self-worth is the key to success in life.
-- Dr. Lise Janelle

In a way, this is the most important section in this book. An entire book can be written on the subject of self-worth, but here we simply touch on the topic and how it relates to creativity.

Self-worth can be described as the confidence in one's own worth or abilities. It is the love or inner value we have for ourselves. Self-worth is our self-image. It is probably more often referred to as self-esteem, but I prefer to use the term self-worth.

Just as images of movies are projected onto the big screen, we project our inner feelings about ourselves upon the external world. The world around us mirrors the way we feel about ourselves. The better we feel about ourselves, the more life around us appears positive, interesting and upbeat. When we do not feel good about ourselves, we are negative, critical and pessimistic about the world and the events in our lives. When we are not feeling worthy, we drag our heels and blame others for what we perceive as misfortunes or tragedies.

Self-worth is the basis for success for everything in life. The key is to believe in yourself: in your worth, abilities and value.

Self-worth is also at the heart of creativity.

Whenever we overcome something we are afraid to do, such as holding a snake, climbing a mountain, writing a book or making a speech, we feel better and stronger and more valuable, and therefore our self-worth increases. Every time we make a promise or commitment to ourselves – and keep it – we feel more inner worth. When we achieve a goal that we set for ourselves, such as increasing financial savings, our self-worth increases. When we toss aside self-doubt and focus energy on what is important to us and aligned with our guiding heart, guess what…we increase our self-worth.

Self-worth equals confidence. Confidence eradicates self-doubt. Negative feelings such as fear, guilt, resentment, anger and jealousy disappear, and we sprout wings and expand the mind. New beginnings arise. Ideas are born. Best of all, we have the self-confidence -- the belief in ourselves -- to manifest them. We begin to shine and achieve great feats.

When we have good self-worth, we take better care of ourselves physically, mentally and spiritually. Conversely, when we take better care of ourselves we have a healthy self-image. We create enriched lives for ourselves and for our loved ones. We see the positive in all situations and are grateful for the beautiful gifts the world offers us on a daily basis. We wake up in the morning and appreciate the sun shining, the birds chirping, or the snow blanketing the ground, and what the rest of the day has in store for us.

When we love ourselves, we create relationships that are good for the heart. We do not remain in relationships because we need to, or feel obligated to, or because we are afraid to leave, or afraid to be alone. Nor do we feel like we are being abandoned. When we are happy and feel good about ourselves, we attract partners who are also happy and feel good about themselves. Joy attracts joy.

Opportunities knock on the doors of people who believe in themselves. And often people who really believe in themselves and their abilities have more money -- much more money. Think of those mega-rich icons that have become household names around the globe, such as Donald Trump or Warren Buffett. These people could not have achieved such enormous wealth or status without believing in themselves.

When we do not feel good about ourselves, we hide in our caves, or crawl under rocks, taking up as little space in the world as possible. If we are in hiding, with no address to be found, how does the Universe know where to send its gifts of opportunities, interesting people and experiences? I have heard it said greatness takes time and space. When we feel good about ourselves, we expand our consciousness and become "bigger." We are certain of our intent. We are not afraid to show the world we are ready, willing and able to provide service. We create more space and attract more gifts, and therefore have more gifts to give.

People who have a good self-image are able to make important life decisions based on inspiration -- what utterly fulfills them -- and do not make decisions from a state of desperation. When we make decisions based on desperation, we are living in a state of basic survival. When

51

we turn to inspiration, we make decisions that are in line with our values and heart. We grow and experience joy along the way. People with self-worth lead inspiring lives attracting fascinating people and exciting opportunities. These are the true leaders of our society. However, whenever we make decisions out of desperation, we constantly doubt ourselves.

Self-worth is at the heart of creativity.
The key is to believe in YOU.

Without self-love, we are without our inner power. When we do not have our inner power, it is difficult to take ideas to the next level and make them a reality.

We all suffer from low self-worth at points in our lives (when we lose a romantic partner, or suffer a business loss, or experience health problems). We can definitely all strive to increase our self-worth. I also believe that life is all about perspective and the choices we make. We can choose to loathe ourselves and experience a difficult and negative life that feels more like a battleground, or we can choose to love ourselves, and experience a life that is beautiful and deeply meaningful. When we choose to love and believe in ourselves, we can make decisions that enable us to reach our desired destination. We want the best for ourselves.

If you are ever doubting yourself, ask yourself important questions that get to the heart of the matter and help change your perspective, such as: What is the *best* thing that could possibly happen from this situation? What is the *worst* thing that could possibly happen? How is this situation helping me get where my heart yearns to go? Where and how far could my wings take me?

It is wise for us to march into our fears, toss aside guilt and attempt to get over negative feelings of resentment, anger, jealously and so forth. These feelings foster self-doubt. And self-doubt does not serve our creative minds.

If obstacles prevent us from living the dreams we desire, or stop us from following through with our ideas and creative projects, those roadblocks are there to teach us important lessons we have not yet learned. They are nothing more than challenges and are meant to help us grow. They are magical gifts from the Universe. When a hurdle arises, the best thing to do is to clearly identify it – then jump it. Take a big leap of faith! Remove the barrier. You will feel better, stronger and believe in yourself, and therefore your creativity will flourish.

Colleen, a young woman who attended one of my workshops, was feeling stuck in her career. She had a day job in a corporation, but she really wanted to be an artist. She had enormous talent, although she never took the steps to create what she desired. She became depressed. After completing my workshop, she was so inspired that she immediately enrolled in a life-drawing class. She suddenly became aware of all the possibilities available to her and the reason she was being held back – the F-word: *fear*. When she told me she had signed up for the drawing class, she had a sparkle in her eye that I will never forget.

When we are living with a purpose and meaning, we love ourselves, have more love for others and experience bliss. When we overcome negative feelings, self-doubt melts away and we feel better about ourselves and therefore take more risks. When we are fully expressing ourselves as creative beings, we increase our self-worth. When we increase our self-worth, we become more creative.

In later chapter in this book are some specific exercises that you can do to help increase your self-worth.

Without self-love, we are without our inner power.

Consider This:

How much do you believe in yourself and your abilities?

The Price of Success

We make a living by what we get.
We make a life by what we give.
-- Winston Churchill

Every goal we set out to achieve has a price tag attached. There is a price to pay for *everything* in life. Success has its price. Having a family has its price. A life of riches and glamour has its price. Living from paycheque to paycheque has its price. Self-employment has its price, but so does working for a corporation. Whatever lifestyle we choose to embrace has its price. Forget the free lunch. Nothing in life is free. There is a price to pay for *everything*, even if it is a hidden cost.

Your dream has its price.

When we look at the big picture, we must determine if we are willing to pay the price to follow our desires. For instance, perhaps you want to start a second career – your dream career – but it may mean taking a salary cut to enable you to dedicate the necessary time. How much is it worth to you? If it means having less money in the short-term it may be worth it. However, if it means financial hardships for years to come forcing you to change your lifestyle, which may have a negative impact on your family, you have a bigger price to pay. Is it still worth it? In the greater scheme of things, if the answer is *yes* -- great! You are living on purpose – zipping down the path you are meant to. If the answer is *no*, it may be time to revisit what gives meaning to your life.

Energy flows where attention goes. If you put all your time and energy into a relationship, you will not have enough time or energy for your creative projects. If you spend all your waking hours working on a creative project, your relationship will suffer because you are not able to put enough energy into it. However, if you share your passion with your mate, you may inspire them to do something in line with their heart. Or by being caught up in your creative project, it will allow your mate to have more time to spend with other family members or friends.

Your creativity has its price.

If you are in a high state of creative flow and work night and day on creating your masterpiece, your social life will pay the price. Maybe to you it is a small price to pay for creating something from your heart. There will always be social life to experience, but if you have that urge to put your energy into your creation, or making your dream come true, you may decide that putting your social life on hold may be worth it (at least for the short term). This is a decision you may be faced with.

If you are working madly day and night on your creation, your physical health may pay the price. At some point, you will be faced with making difficult choices.

If you are afraid to make decisions that will enable you to follow your creative desires, *that decision alone has its price*. For instance, by not listening to your whispering heart, you may become depressed and experience health problems, or relationship problems.

What price are you willing to pay to follow your creative dream, and live with joy and fulfillment? What price are you willing to pay if you do *not* follow your dream?

Reframing "Success"

From the beginning of time, people around the world have given up something to follow their dreams. These people have achieved success, regardless of whether it made them financially rich or not. They are successful because at the very least they *overcame self-doubt*. Ultimately, they lived their lives and followed a dream, no matter the outcome. They paid the price for success and, I hazard to guess, if you had the opportunity to ask them they would likely say it was worthwhile.

Fame has its price tag, too. Movie star Marlon Brando was known to have remarked, "Fame is a curse." I think any celebrity, whether a Hollywood actor, musician, business tycoon, writer and the like, pays the biggest price of all for their creative dreams. To be in the public eye constantly must be extremely taxing, especially in those moments of public humiliation, regardless of whether it is a relationship break-up, drug problem or being slammed by the critics for a poor performance. While glamorous to many people on the outside, being in the limelight must be gruelling. Consider superstars Michael Jackson, Nicole

Kidman, Tom Cruise, Martha Stewart, and the former "king of rock and roll," Elvis Presley. Think of the unrelenting international media attention their lives have generated. I can only imagine how difficult it is for families and friends of superstars, and how it must impact their own physical and emotional health.

If you dream of being famous, or are infatuated with the notion, consider the price you will have to pay once you reach that destination. Fame will inevitably have a *big* price tag attached. For some people fame makes them want to shrivel up and become small. Others thrive off it. What's more, you cannot tell one from the other based on their public personas. It is only in the intimacy of their private lives that this may be obvious (unless, of course, they go public about their feelings). Think of the superstars who took their own lives, such as Marilyn Monroe and Nirvana's Kurt Cobain. To the external world, these people had it all – fame, success, glamour -- but really they were feeling quite opposite in their hearts. To see them in public one would not have known *they did not feel successful as a person.*

The search for fame for fame's sake may be a way of numbing poor self-worth and is not a balanced state to be in. Many people seek fame to make them be whole and important. If people are not feeling balanced before being famous, fame will inevitably spin them off their centres even more. Wanting to express creative genius is a worthy cause that may lead to fame as a by-product -- this is a healthy state for us. Otherwise, people who want fame to make them feel better about themselves often crash when they discover that fame, alas, does not bring happiness.

And so, if you dream of fame, ask yourself if you are willing to pay the enormous price attached to it. But first ask yourself *why* you want to be famous to begin with.

In terms of being successful in life, what is important is to define success not by society's values or by comparison to other people, or whether you achieve fame, but to define success *according to your own values.*

Success truly is a matter of the perspective you choose to take. If you decide you are going to fail, guess what…you fail. If you decide you are going to achieve, guess what…you achieve.

The key is to make decisions not out of self-doubt, fear, guilt, resentment, anger, jealousy or desperation, but *make decisions out of love for yourself and what inspires your whispering heart.* When you take this perspective, you experience a life of joy and meaning. This is true success.

With regard to your dreams, chances are the satisfaction and joy you glean from the creative process alone is juicy enough of a reward. The bottom line is this: you cannot lose! Regardless of whether a creative project gets finished or an idea goes to market or a manuscript gets published, you have much to gain by just *enjoying the creative process.* Throughout the process, you learn about yourself and feel joy while exploring your creativity and living the life you choose.

This is when you are successful.

Look and you will find it -- what is unsought will go undetected.
-- Sophocles

Give This a Whirl:

What is your definition of success? Write a paragraph or two about what success means to you.

Ignite Inspiration

I shut my eyes in order to see.
-- Paul Gauguin

Inspiration is the gasoline of life. Discover what inspires you for it fuels your drive to dream up ideas and new ways of experiencing life. Ignite your inspiration. When you are inspired, it naturally leads to creation. Being inspired is like delightfully nibbling on chocolate: it leaves you desiring more.

Where does one find inspiration?

Well, that is personal.

Inspiration is all around us, anxiously waiting to be discovered. It is skulking around with friends, cuddling with family members and soaking up the sun in the backyard. Inspiration is scrawled on the blackboards at school, giggling on the swings at the park, wearing lampshades at parties, swimming in the sea, and plunked on top of a mountain. Inspiration is hiding deep in our closets and cupboards. It is sleeping in the old tickle trunk filled with memorabilia such as photo albums and home movies. Actually, I will take the plunge and suggest...*where is inspiration not?*Inspiration is within you...and all around you.

What inspires you? Maybe you already know. If you are not sure, or are seeking ideas, read on. There are many different ways to find inspiration:

Connect With Inspiring People

By being close to inspiring people we become inspired through hearing their dreams and stories of achievement. Their inspiration rubs off like gold dust and we may find doors opening for us. It is beneficial to connect with inspiring people as often as possible. If you do not know people you consider inspiring source them out. Hang out where inspiring people hang out. Try film and music festivals, seminars, workshops, cooking classes, speaking engagements, art shows, cocktail parties, your place of employment. Search the Internet, including chat rooms. Ask friends for suggestions. Look in your neighborhood. You will inevitably find a few of them working madly over a cup of java at a coffee shop, guaranteed.

Personally, I find that writing in a coffee shop is a terrific way to connect with other writers. I enjoy hearing about the other writers' projects, lending a compassionate ear, or being a cheerleader to help keep them motivated and trucking along their paths. It helps to keep me inspired, and sometimes I need a compassionate ear and a few hardy cheers myself.

Another place I connect with inspiring people on a regular basis is, of all places, the dog park. My neighborhood in Toronto is filled with inspiring, creative people who, like me, routinely take their dogs to the park. Every day I bump into film and television producers, directors, actors, writers, editors, designers, entrepreneurs, artists, restaurant and shop owners, musicians, business executives, stay-at-home moms, and so on. It is an excellent place to chat with a variety of inspiring people and learn about their creative projects, dreams and achievements -- and it is free-of-charge.

Learn About Famous "Creatives"

Choose famous creative people whom you admire and take the time to learn about them. Perhaps, like me, you fancy famous "creatives" like Peter Gabriel, Meryl Streep, Katharine Hepburn and Vincent van Gogh. To get your juices flowing, here are other examples of famous creatives: Bob Hope, Helen Keller, Beethoven, Mozart, Dorothy Parker, Denzel Washington, Shakespeare, Charlie Chaplin and David Bowie. What do they all have in common? What do you have in common with them?

The best way to learn about famous creative people is to *read* about them. Pick up biographical books on people you admire and read about their challenges, heartaches, dreams, triumphs and, most importantly, the keys to their success. Read interviews in newspapers and magazines. Pay close attention to their challenges (they all have them) and how they overcame those challenges. Learn from their experiences: the good and the bad. Bookstores and libraries have large collections of biographies (books and tapes) of many interesting people who have lead fascinating lives. Many are rags to riches stories, which are inspiring. Famous creatives are superb human examples to remind us that anything is possible.

Bookstore bargain tables are like gold mines for information on famous creatives. Whenever I am craving or begging for inspiration, I make my way to a bargain table for a random browsing adventure. I find bargain tables filled with loads of material about inspiring people that I might otherwise not consider or care about. I usually leave with a flurry of new ideas.

Another wonderful way to learn about famous creative people is to watch television programs such as *Biography* (on A&E) and documentaries. Documentaries are becoming more and more popular and accessible to the public, and are a terrific way to experience someone else's life, and a little slice of history. Some of the big budget documentaries make it to the big screen, but mostly you will find documentary films in local video stores (find one that has a decent selection) or on television.

Some radio shows also offer interesting interviews with fascinating people.

If you do not have a lot of time on your hands, a quick way of learning about famous creative people is to source out information on the Internet. Many famous creatives have their own dedicated websites. You may also find information through related industry sites, fan sites, or by doing a global search.

Be Self-Motivated

If inspiration is the gasoline of life, *self-motivation* is the electricity. It is extremely important to be self-motivated. As the popular motivational speaker Zig Ziglar aptly noted, "People often say that motivation doesn't last. Well, neither does bathing – that's why we recommend it daily. " Just like your daily bathing, be motivated every day. By connecting with other people who are motivated it helps us to be more motivated, inspired – and squeaky clean. You are the "soul" driver of your creative project. It is totally up to you to find your way to the gas station for that fuel that keeps you moving forward along your journey. If you lose motivation, do what you can to muster up the energy to find a way to ignite the spark (please be sure to stay clear of the gas pump!). The *best* way to stay motivated is to hang around inspiring people, or to read about and listen to their stories.

- *One exercise that works well to stay motivated is to write down all the pros of seeing your project through to the end and the cons of not seeing your project through to the end. How do you envision it unfolding or turning out? What are the benefits of completing it? What are the drawbacks if you do not complete it? This exercise can be helpful to keep the fire burning.*

Collaborate With Others

Consider collaborating on projects with people who have similar interests, even if it is a small or one-off project. This is a great way to connect with passionate people, work on a variety of projects, and keep each other inspired and motivated. My advice is to seek out people who complement your talents, who may have strengths or resources where your feel you have weaknesses or lack of resources. The key is to work with people you admire, trust, are motivated and hold similar values.

Also, depending on your interests, consider joining a special interest group: a forum where you can share your ideas and interests, such as a book or movie club, writer's group, poet's circle, woodworker's anonymous, Toastmaster's, etc. The size of the group does not matter – aim for quality. When people share interests in a group setting, energy and momentum tends to build, which leads to creation. Inevitably, group members keep each other inspired and motivated.

Suzanne Falter-Barns, author of *How Much Joy Can You Stand*, seems to have a good thing happening with her inspirational "joy groups," which she has organized across North America. If you are interested, check out if there is a "joy group" in your neighborhood.

Get a Mentor

Another terrific source for inspiration is a *mentor*. Mentors are key to keeping dreams alive, getting valuable advice and, when needed, giving us a gentle "get your rear in gear" nudge. Find at least one mentor; someone you admire and respect who is accomplished at what you desire to achieve. Mentors provide us with guidance and encourage us to grow and stay motivated. Mentors also keep us humble, especially when we begin to become cocky about our talents (there is always something more to learn). We could have several mentors for different areas of life. Also consider investing in a *life coach*: these "paid mentors" are all the rage today and worth the investment in yourself.

When you feel confident and experienced, take on a student and pass along your inspiration and knowledge to them. There is an excellent reason for this: students increase our self-worth, providing a point of reference for our own growth from which we began our journey. And we evolve and have even more to offer others.

Qualities to look for in a mentor:

1. *They are accomplished at what you desire to achieve.*

2. *They are professional.*

3. *They are self-motivated and encourage you to be motivated.*

4. *You trust them and the advice they offer.*

5. *They are accessible to you, even if it isa quick telephone call or e-mail.*

6. *You feel they have your best interest at heart.*

Be Inspired from the Whispering Heart

When inspiration comes from the heart it leads to creation and joy. When we are inspired from the heart, we desire to build, to grow, to try something new, to explore, to love. We stop creating when we "fall out of" inspiration. When we lose interest, we lose steam and our momentum crashes. Let your ideas come from the heart rather than *ego*. *Ego kills creativity.* When coming from the heart, your ideas are true to your life's purpose and inevitably those ideas become reality.

- *Whenever something or someone inspires you, pay attention to what happens next. Keep track of these events in a calendar or journal.*

Connect with Nature

Draw inspiration from nature, either working on creative projects or relaxing your mind and recharging your spirit. Connecting with nature is inspirational at best, pleasurable at worst. In today's busy world, we are constantly distracted by noise pollution, social activity and obligations. Our houses morph into Grand Central Station. Offices are abuzz with hyper communication and electronic screeching. With so much distraction, the connection to the soul becomes clouded and twisted. By unplugging and connecting with nature, we connect with our soul, the whispers of our heart, and we allow the mind to expand. We simply become more creative.

For city dwellers...do not fret! Options are available. Consider renting, buying or borrowing a cottage. Or check out retreats designed for writers and other artists. Take an extended vacation to a country where you can survive on little money for a long period of time. Or stay with a friend or relative who resides in an inspiring location. If your budget is tight, create your own peaceful space in a garden, or your background, or on a rooftop. Or get involved in a community garden project. One of my personal favorites: relaxing at a park with an inspiring book and my dog on a sunny Sunday afternoon.

One of my city friends built a small studio in her backyard. It is a miniature one-room cottage, the size of a storage shed, but it is a wonderful place where she can disappear anytime she wants to write and not be bothered. Sitting in her studio, one would not realize they are in the centre of a buzzing metropolis. While this may not be a possibility for everyone, I include it here as an example of what *is* possible.

Check Out Museums, Art Shows, Galleries, Theatres

Whenever you get the opportunity check out museums, art and

craft shows, galleries, theatres and other cultural places oozing with inspiration. Spend an afternoon at an art museum enjoying the creativity of the great masters, such as Rodin and Rembrandt. Said Michelangelo, "The marble not yet carved can hold the form of every thought the greatest artist has." Connect with the mastery of the masters. Grasp their journey; turn it into your destiny. The shops at museums and galleries are also inspirational and not to be missed.

If money is tight, source out the *free* art and craft shows, art shops and pay-what-you-can theatrical performances. Museums usually have a designated time when they are open to the public free-of-charge. One does not necessarily need a lot of money to do these activities, a detail many people often overlook.

Special occasions are great opportunities to share the experience with a friend or family member. For instance, on your birthday shut down your computer and spend the afternoon with a friend at a museum. Make it a gift to yourself. And consider making it a habit of purchasing at least one inspiring book every time you visit a gallery or museum to add to your library.

Create a "Wow" Inspiring Space

Make your *home and work environment* inspirational in a style personal to you. Enhance your space in ways that please the senses and turn it into a place that is not only inspiring to you, but also inspiring to others. Make the space so interesting when people walk in the door they bellow, "Wow!"

Collect artefacts or interesting objects, such a coloured glass or seashells, that have meaning to you and place them in your work area. Play music that speaks to your soul. Paint the walls outlandish colours, or calming ones. I personally enjoy collecting tribal masks from around the world. My walls are also covered with vibrant artwork and photos from my travels to far-away places, which constantly keep me inspired and my memories of inspiring places and times fresh. I listen to jazz or classical music while writing, and when I am in the mood I also enjoy burning scented candles. As well, I find working near a window where I am able to watch the world go by makes a difference in my energy level.

A creative environment lends itself well to a creative mind. Take into consideration:

- **Colour** *has different effects on mood, which impacts our creativity. There are many books written about decor and the use of colour to create mood. Check out home-improvement television shows, if you are inclined. Use colour in a way that works best for you. As an example, if you want an "energetic" feel, consider painting your space combinations of orange and yellow. We'll explore colour in a later chapter.*
- **Music** *affects brainwave patterns, helping us to learn, remember and, of course, relax. Classical music especially impacts creative thinking. For an exploration of music and its benefits, I recommend reading The Mozart Effect: Tapping the Power of Music to Heal the Body, Strengthen the Mind and Unlock the Creative Spirit by Don Campbell.*
- **Sunshine** *has a major impact on our energy level. Spend as much time as possible in sunshine and pay attention to the way low seasonal light affects you. If you are badly affected by low seasonal light it will impact your creativity, therefore you may want to consider making adjustments, such as getting a full-spectrum light or spending more time in the sunshine. If you are seriously affected, taking drastic measures such as moving to a sunny destination may be worth the effort.*

Get Sparked by Sports and Recreational Activities

Some people draw inspiration from doing extreme sports such as heli-skiing and rock climbing. Not my cup of tea, mind you, but it could be yours! I can certainly imagine and appreciate how inspiring it is to sit on top of Mount Everest at sunrise with a view of the beautiful earth as far as the eye can see. There are very few people who have or will ever experience this moment in their lifetime, and so if you dream of it...go for it! Of course, other sports that are not so extreme can also be inspiring, such as playing hockey, tennis or rowing.

If you are not into extreme sports, maybe more leisurely recreational activities such as sailing, canoeing, hiking, cycling, skating, downhill and cross-country skiing, and snowshoeing for those residing in the snowy north, are apt to do the trick.

These kinds of sports and leisurely activities are not only inspirational; they also help to develop self-confidence and keep us physically fit and active.

Everything is Connected

We are all part of the fabric that makes up the expansive Universe. We are also *all* connected through our thoughts and our actions. Pay attention to the *connections* in this world that appear to be miracles or magic. Making new business contacts by "fluke" is one example. Bumping into a film producer who "just so happens" to be looking for your kind of script is another. So is getting a call "out of the blue" from a childhood friend you were just thinking about.

These kinds of connections are marvelously inspirational. Some people believe in fate and others believe we create our own destiny. Many believe everything happens for a reason and that we are all connected. Some believe in miracles and magic. If you open yourself up to this way of experiencing the world, your creativity opens up as well.

**When you love what you do and do what you love,
You love yourself for it.
The journey begins with inspiration.**

Give These a Whirl:

1. *Write a list of your major creative achievements over your lifetime, as far back as you can recall. Perhaps you took a stab at a short story, or a painting, or appeared in a commercial. Maybe you came up with a great idea for a new product and developed a plan to make it a reality. How have these achievements helped guide you to where*

you dream of going? Remind yourself how well you are presently doing by updating your list on a regular basis (such as weekly or monthly). It is a great way of giving yourself a self-worth boost.

2. *Write a list of famous creative people you admire. What is it about these people that makes them creative? Successful? Why do you admire them? What do they all have in common? What do you have in common with them? Learn about them and connect with their journey (read biographies and feature articles; watch television shows and documentaries). How can you apply that information to your own journey?*

3. *Spend at least one hour every day for one week doing a variety of activities that are inspirational to you, or trying new activities that you believe you may find inspiring. In a calendar, mark down the activities you did, on the day you did them, and note any insights you may have experienced. See how it changes your energy and drive over the course of a few months.*

4. *Read about, hang around, listen to, and watch people who are inspiring to you – as much as humanly possible.*

67

Be an Inspiring Person

The best way to cheer yourself up
is to try to cheer somebody else up.
-- Mark Twain

Be an inspiring person and doors of opportunity open. Strive to open your heart and listen to what your heart whispers to you. When you follow the wisdom of your whispering heart, you will live an inspiring life, attract people with the same energy, and inspire other people to do the same. It's catchy!

Some of the messages in this section were touched on earlier, but they are so critically important they bear repeating here *because this is what will help you become an inspiring person.*

The way we open the heart is to transcend negative feelings that ultimately lead to or foster self-doubt. How we transcend these negative feelings is to live with *gratitude*. When we live with gratitude and see all the positives or benefits in life, the whispering heart opens. When the heart opens, we have more self-love and begin to believe in our abilities. Self-doubt melts away and we create meaningful lives that touch the hearts of others.

It may sound impossible right now that I would ask you to be grateful for something you feel was bad for you, and it may sound a bit crazy, too. But, from my own experience and the experience of thousands of other people who have integrated this gratitude principle into their lives, when you get a bigger picture of the situation and realize how something that you felt was only bad *also* came with some benefits, or some experiences that you benefited from, consequently it takes away negative feelings such as anger and resentment.

The best way to understand this is to ask yourself: "What would have been the drawbacks to me if I did *not* have this person or situation in my life?" By asking this question outright, and discovering the answer, you can see how the person or situation helped you grow and learn, and *that perspective* helps steer your heart in the direction it yearns to go. When you do this, you will live with more gratitude and therefore create an inspiring life.

And so, be an inspiring person and create an inspiring vibe. By doing

68

this, you attract people with the same energy and inspire others to become inspiring themselves. In this next section we explore how.

Open Your Heart with Gratitude

Here are a number of ways you can live with love and gratitude *every day*:

- *To feel grateful for a person or an event that pushes your buttons, write out a list of all the "benefits" (big or small) this person or situation gives you. Keep going until you have exhausted all the benefits and experience heartfelt gratitude – however long it takes. By determining all benefits, we develop a healthy, balanced perspective, and negativity slips away. When you see all the benefits, your heart opens up – to yourself and to others.*

- *Love unconditionally. No matter what, keep your heart open to loved ones and people who mean a lot to you. Love them for who they are. It does not mean you have to keep people in your life who should not be in it, or remain in situations not healthy for you, but find gratitude for those people and situations, and keep your heart open – even if you must say good-bye. Above all, love yourself.*

- *Be "in the moment" with your loved ones and people important to you when in their presence. Give them respect and pay attention to what they have to say.*

- *Just before retiring to bed each night, take a moment to write down everything you are grateful for that day including people, events, feelings, magical "gifts," etc.*

- *Whatever or whomever you are grateful for, be aware of it and let your heart embrace it. By feeling grateful, we are being loving, and we can transcend any negative thoughts or feelings we have.*

- *Tell the people close to you that you are grateful for them whenever you can, daily if possible. You may be grateful for the small things they do, for their love, for their precious time, for their wisdom, for lending a compassionate ear, for their gifts. Whatever it is, communicate your feelings of gratitude.*

- *Send good thoughts to those people who you are unable to speak with due to distance. As well, be sure to send good thoughts to people you do not like or feel have done you wrong.*

Believe in Yourself by Increasing Your Self-Worth

As Dr. Janelle says in her *Inward Bound* personal growth seminar: "The world around us reflects the self-worth we have. The more self-worth we have the more worth is reflected around us and the more beautiful our life seems."

As I discovered along my own personal journey, and the many other people around the world who have integrated these same principles into their lives, learning to love oneself is hard work and is a life-long process. But, it is crucial to being able to believe in your worth and abilities, and to achieve success in a way that is meaningful to you. What is important is to take the *action steps* necessary to feel not just good -- but great -- about yourself. When you do this, you can turn any dream you have into reality.

There are a number of ways to go about increasing your self-worth:

1.   Discover Your Life's Purpose

The first step in increasing self-worth is to take yourself on a journey of self-exploration. A good jump off point is to know with certainty and clarity who you are and what your purpose in life is (what gives you joy and meaning every day). If we do not know with certainty and clarity who we are and what our purpose is, how do we know if we are on the right path? How would we know if we are making the best decisions for us? How would we recognize the best opportunities for us when they knock at the door? It is wise for us to spend the time and energy discovering or re-discovering who we are and what our purpose in life is. And as you grow, so will your life's purpose. It evolves with you.

- *Spend a moment thinking about your life's purpose. Your purpose is what gives you joy and meaning every day, and it is not just about work/career. Write down a few paragraphs about your purpose (a "statement of purpose") and commit it to memory. Specifically, write out what you want "to be," "to do," and "to have." Borrowing from the Inward Bound principles, incorporate aspects from all seven areas of life: career, finance, family, social, spiritual, mental and physical.*

Here is an example of a "statement of purpose" that you could tailor to your own life if you wish: My purpose in life is "to be" a fully loving individual who lives with courage, wisdom, gratitude and creative expression. My "to do" is to provide excellent service in business (or job), spend time with my loved ones, dedicate myself to growth, and inspire other people to do the same. By doing these things that matter deeply to my heart, I want "to have" health, knowledge, wisdom, prosperity and abundant love.

Since your life's purpose will continue to evolve as you do, consider updating what you have written periodically to keep it fresh and current.

2. Love Your Strengths and Weaknesses

As part of this journey of self-exploration, it is wise to identify all your strengths and weaknesses. Then take *ownership* of them. Really own each one of them. Love them all. Once you identify all your strengths and weaknesses, take a close look at your "perceived" weaknesses. How do they actually serve you as *strengths*, rather than weaknesses? How are your perceived strengths actually *weaknesses*?

We all have strengths and weaknesses, and to have both is a perfect balance. See the perfection in having both. Learn to love your weaknesses for they help you grow. When you see two sides of the same coin, you have the whole picture and a perspective that is healthy and balanced.

For instance, being a "perfectionist" can be a strength, but it also can be a weakness. Being a "clean freak" is a strength *and* weakness. Being

71

"thrifty" is a strength *and* weakness. Being "loyal" has its strengths and weaknesses. It all depends on situations and circumstances…and perspective.

3.   *Spend Time Alone*

One of the best ways of plumbing the core of your creative essence is to spend time alone. Not only is it difficult to be highly creative when other people are around, by spending time alone we connect with our heart and soul and deepest desires. When we spend time alone we discover our ambitions, tastes, desires, fears, abilities and dreams. Avoid distraction and spend time alone working on creative projects whenever possible. Or spend time relaxing or "exploring" on your own.

Consider the following:

* *Devise a schedule that allows you to have alone time.*

* *Make a date with yourself to "hang out" now and again.*

* *Consider taking a vacation alone, even if it is for a short weekend.*

* *Hang a "Do Not Disturb" sign on your office or bedroom door.*

* *Hire a sitter to take care of children or a pet while you take a break.*

4.   *Record Your Heart Whispers*

Record what your heart whispers to you in a journal, notepad or on recycled scraps of paper if you must; or use a small tape recorder. Take note of important thoughts, feelings, insights, fears, dreams, aspirations and events. Revisit it occasionally if you wish to use it as a point of reference for your personal growth.

It is also advisable to carry a small notebook around with you to write down things that inspire you such as ideas, quotations, interesting facts, names to remember, books to read, movies to see, places to go, and so forth. Ideas have wings, so it is best to jot them down as soon as they pop up so you do not forget them.

5.   *Project a Good Self-Image*

F _ _ K!
Bad language, bad image.

Become aware of the image you project to the outside world. If you are pleased with the image you project, great! If you are not projecting the image you want, you may need to make adjustments. It is wise to learn to project a *good self-image*. How do you dress? How do you carry yourself? How do you walk in those high heels? How do you articulate your thoughts? In particular, our vocabulary says heaps about our self-image. Therefore use vocabulary that reflects the image you wish to project. I do not mean you must use the Queen's English either. If we curse like drunken sailors, we are viewed like drunken sailors. If we speak with confidence, we are viewed as being confident.
    Let me ask you this: how do you want to be perceived by others?

An intelligent person?
A powerful person?
A successful person?
An important person?
An inspiring person?

It is important to know the mind makes powerful connections between what we say and think, and how we perceive our reality. To help put it into context, ask yourself: "How would an inspiring person think?" Then think what an inspiring person would think. Or ask yourself: "What would an important person say?" Then say what an important person would say.
    As a suggestion, adopt the image of a mentor. You do not have to be a copycat, but take a lesson or two from how they present themselves.

73

How do they dress? Are they articulate? How do they organize their time? How energy-efficient are they? How do they express their desires, plans and ideas?

- *Try This: Pick three people you know and trust. Ask each of them to describe your image.*

6. Meditate On It

Meditation also helps us to discover ourselves, believe in our abilities and therefore be inspirational. Meditation helps to access and develop the brain waves that take us into a deeper state of consciousness and relaxation. Here, in this deep state, we connect with the soul. We become more aware of our heart's whispers, our thoughts and visions. Not only is meditation excellent for attaining an optimistic outlook, it is beneficial to use it as a means to develop visual images for creative projects. It is a great way to develop characters and plots, and to dream up new business ventures and ways of living. Once you start meditating and feel the amazing benefits, you will be hooked for life.

Tips for meditation:

1. *Try to meditate at the same time daily. Early morning is best.*

2. *Find a quiet place, away from distractions.*

3. *Sit comfortably (if you lie down you will fall asleep) with eyes closed.*

4. *Do not meditate when your stomach is full or you will feel sleepy.*

5. *Breathe in and out slowly, and calm your mind.*

6. *In your mind, go to a comfortable place (a room, bed, comfy chair, enchanted garden). Spend time in this magical place working through creative solutions, ideas, and relationship problems – whatever you wish.*

7. *Continue to breathe deeply and stay focussed throughout your meditation.*

8. *Start with short sessions (say 5 minutes) and eventually work your way to longer sessions (half-hour to an hour or longer).*

9. *If the phone rings, let it go into voice mail. They can wait.*

10. *After your meditation, record any insights or ideas that occur.*

If the notion of sitting quietly for a period of time is disconcerting to you, instead go for walks, write in a journal, sit peacefully on a beach watching waves break, or plunk yourself on a park bench. These are all terrific ways to meditate. Find a means of quietening the mind that works best for you.

7. *Talk to the Universe with Prayer*

You may have heard it said: meditation is listening to the Universe and prayer is *talking* to it. Incorporate *prayer* into your daily routine in whatever way that is personal and meaningful to you. I do not mean prayer in a religious sense either. I suggest finding a way to express your deepest desires, appreciation, gratitude and concerns to the Universe. Talk to the Universe, to the stars, to the big entity in the sky, to your God. Never be afraid to ask for what you want. Just prepare to receive it.

When I was a child I was taught to say a wee prayer before I went to sleep that began with the words: "Now I lay me down to sleep…" I remember the warm and fuzzy feeling that overtook me every night I said my prayer, and how my imagination wandered far, far away. Throughout my teens and my early adult years, I stopped praying as I became one without religion and I viewed prayer as a religious act.

Later in my adult years, I re-discovered the power of prayer in a way that is meaningful to me. Every night, just like when I was five years old, when my head hits the pillow I say my wee prayer. However, it no longer begins with the same words I used as a child. I take a minute to talk to the Universe and express my heart and soul. I still get that warm and fuzzy feeling I had as a child, and it still sparks my imagination, while giving me hope, courage and gratitude. Find prayer in a way that suits you and, if you have not done so already, discover the power associated with it.

8. *Visualize the Life You Desire*

Visualization gets us beyond self-doubt and into a state of certainty and clarity. Imagine yourself as the inspiring person you would love to be: an artist, writer, cabinet-maker, opera singer, designer, senior executive, entrepreneur, parent. Imagine living the life you desire. Then imagine how you can impact and inspire other people. When you begin to feel shaky about your goals or are experiencing self-doubt thoughts, return to the same visualization for a self-worth boost. Visualize the life you want to lead. Visualization helps to increase our self-worth and propels us forward. If all else fails, fake it 'til you make it. Honest, it works!

- *Spend a few minutes visualizing yourself living an inspiring life, being an inspiring person. Do you see yourself as an actor in children's television programs? Or how about a sought-after inventor? A teacher? Are you surrounded by lots of family and loved ones? Are you in a house by the sea? Are you a multi-billionaire who uses her/his money to help others reach their human potential?*

9. *Blow Your Mind, Think Big*

Expand your consciousness beyond your current limits and think BIG, and therefore BE BIG. Expand your vision as much as you possibly can. See yourself as someone who can achieve great things that impact other people in a beneficial way. If you think big, you grow big. By expanding your consciousness and vision you can and will make an impact on society with your creativity, and inspire others along the way.

But know that regardless of whatever size your dream is, it is good size that is right for you. It is not the size that counts the most. What is truly important is to feel "proud" of your dream and where you are at with it. Just give it your best shot. By following your dream, regardless of the size, others become inspired.

Like so many other famous recording artists, Neil Young left Canada when he was a lad for the exciting music scene of Los Angeles, a place where, in his heart, he felt he could impact many more people with his music. He had a big vision and believed in himself enough to follow it. He is living proof that it works.

10.   Listen to Intuition

Get gutsy and go with your intuition...you know, that inkling or hunch you get now and again. Listen to your sixth sense (the word *intuition* is Latin for "in to you").

Intuition does not explain itself to us. Rather, its job is merely *to point the way*. Learn to identify it, trust it and know how it benefits you. There are books you can read to help you understand what intuition is and how to use it. Mostly, if you just listen to your heart and tune into your soul you have the answers. Be sure to take notes from any insights you may have and refer to them from time to time.

Forms that intuition can take:

- *subtle inkling, hunch, gut feeling*

- *strong, obvious messages that whack you across the head*

- *symbols and visual images*

- *actual words*

- *experience deeper meaning*

- *dreams*

11. Own Your Intention

Part of being an inspiring person is to take *responsibility* for your dream and *own your intention*. Responsibility is about maturity; and there is power in intention. Gandhi had powerful intent. So does Madonna. So does the president of the United States. Books get published, films get made, plays get produced and products go to market because of intent.

What is your intention? Be clear on what you intend to do and state it to the Universe, or your God, as well as other people close to you. That way, everyone is reading from the same page. Walk your talk and it will increase your self-worth and inspire others. Incorporate your intentions into your daily prayers, if you wish. Or write down your intentions on paper. If you find yourself wobbling with what you intend on doing, revisit what you have written. Be proud of what you intend to achieve and be sure to own it. There is a lot of power in intention...so, what do you intend to do?

12.   Strive to Do Your Best

Strive to do your best every day and be inspiring to others. Provide the best service possible to clients, employers or whoever engages your services. At the end of the day, ask yourself if you have given your best service. If you have, great! You will feel good about yourself for it and it will make you feel and be more productive. If, for whatever reason, you were not able to give your best, do not feel bad. Instead, make a promise to yourself to do your best the following day.

Keep in mind whenever you make a promise to yourself – and keep it – your self-worth increases and you feel more successful. Strive for excellence and you inspire others...even if it means taking baby steps to get you there.

10 Ways to provide excellent service:

- *Anticipate the needs of clients (or the boss, or partner).*

- *Return telephone calls and e-mails promptly (unless during "off limits" time when you are creating).*

- *Deliver "the goods" on or before deadlines.*

- *Do not "over promise," but "over deliver" wherever possible.*

- *Aim for quality work.*

- *Hit your spell check button before sending documents or e-mails.*

- *Be accountable.*

- *Use time wisely and productively.*

- *Honesty has a lot of value.*

- *Be grateful for people who critique your work, for they help you grow.*

13.   *Be Patient, Gain Wisdom*

You probably heard the old adage: patience is a virtue. Like me, maybe your mother incorporated that into her daily lecture series while you were growing up. However, have you ever wondered *why* patience is considered a virtue? *Patience is wisdom.* Take a look at any senior citizen within your social circle and listen to the wise words they so often utter: be patient.

When it comes to your creative endeavours, learn to enjoy the journey and not just the desired results. There is joy in the creative process and you learn about yourself along the way, and while travelling this road you touch the hearts of others. Be patient, because fulfillment does not happen overnight. When you are dealing with creative pursuits and living out dreams, you are most definitely in for the long haul before true fulfillment is possible. Once you are fulfilled and experiencing joy, you inspire other people to do the same. It is worth the wait. Honest.

How does one find more patience?

- *Be grateful for what you have and who you are right now.*

- *Look at how everything happens for a reason: discover how/ why the things that are happening at the moment (good and bad) are helping you get what you want.*

- *Stay calm amidst chaos.*

- *Prepare for the worst outcome, plan for the best.*

- *Discover all the benefits in going through the creative process itself.*

- *Set reasonable goals.*

- *Use meditation and visualization techniques.*

- *Put your trust in the Universe, or your God.*

14. Rewire Thinking Patterns with Affirmations

Reciting affirmations several times every day is a highly valuable tool to rewire your thinking patterns in a way that is positive and powerful. Find a book with examples of affirmations if you must, although it is better if you develop your own because it uses your creative thinking. Post your affirmations around your house on sticky notes. Stick them on your refrigerator, computer screen or bathroom mirror.

Affirmations are positive and powerful statements that keep us believing in ourselves. Reciting them is about taking action toward your dream. They often begin with "I am" or "I have," but not necessarily.

Here are some examples of affirmations to try:

- *I am a creative genius who follows her/his heart.*

- *I am a healthy, wealthy artist who aims to love.*

- *By living my creative dream, I am successful.*

- *I have the power to create.*

- *I love what I do and I do what I love.*

- *I am an accomplished (fill in the blank).*

- *I am powerful.*

- *I am a good person.*

Say these affirmations to yourself whenever you can. Say them over and over and over again. You may feel silly at first walking around the house saying "I am a creative genius," or "I am an accomplished pianist," especially if loved ones are around, or a pet. My favourite place to recite affirmations is in the shower, on walks, or sitting comfortably on my bed just before I go to sleep (that way, positive thoughts get filed in my brain and pulled out the next morning). Sometimes I even say my affirmations to my dog; he just tilts his head with a "yeah, whatever" expression. Discover what place and time works best for you.

If you are stuck creatively and keep reciting your affirmations, eventually you believe in yourself, you grow and your creativity soars. Amazing things unfold. Once you get into the good habit of reciting affirmations that are deeply meaningful to you, and experience the benefits they bring, you are hooked for life.

15. Use of Language

Garbage in…garbage out…watch thy mouth! Negative language can wreak havoc on our subconscious thoughts and impact our creativity ever so slowly, like a leak in a tire. Even if you do not know it, your tire continues to leak air and eventually you go *flat.*

You may have heard the analogy used that our subconscious is like a *filing cabinet,* storing all sorts of information from how we feel during special romantic moments, to the seeds of our fears. Our vocabulary has an impact on what goes in and out of our filing cabinet. It certainly can impact creativity, directly or indirectly. For instance, if you keep saying you do not have the ability to paint, that negative "document" gets placed in your filing cabinet and pulled out now and again to ensure you never have the ability to paint.

You may need to rewire your brain to change the way you use language. It is important to choose positive language. Use words that convey certainty and determination. Be assertive. Show the world you mean business. For instance: "<u>When</u> I finish my novel" *instead* of "<u>If</u> I finish my novel." There is a big difference between "when and if." Another example: "I <u>am making time</u> to write" *versus* "I <u>do not have time</u> to write."

Spend time paying attention to language; the language you use as well as the language used by people close to you. Garbage in, garbage out! If the people you surround yourself with use negative, self-doubting language, inevitably it impacts you one way or another. You, too, will use self-doubting language, which only decreases your self-worth and holds you back from being highly creative. Again, it works like a slow leak in a tire.

One popular negative phrase that prevents us from achieving our creative potential is: "I'll never earn a living." Actually, there are several variations of that including: "Artists do not make money," or "I've got bills to pay so I cannot take a chance." There are people from all over the world who earn a living from being creative and are highly successful. *What we envisage we become.*

Follow Your Whispering Heart

Now that you know the underlying keys to achieving success: live with an open heart and gratitude, and develop good self-worth, you can make decisions from the heart that are liberating. Your heart whispers its desires and, without fail, it tells you what is right for you. You gain wisdom as well as creative freedom. When you follow your heart you feel successful. By following your whispering heart, other people find you inspiring and they, too, will follow their hearts.

If we make decisions because we are feeling "desperate," like giving up a dream to find a menial job to pay the bills in order to get by, we are in basic survival mode. We are not necessarily making the best decisions for the heart. If you are making decisions from a place of desperation, it can lead to depression because you are not fulfilling your heart's desires. In this situation, the sense of a lack of freedom of spirit often develops.

When we live with gratitude, we transcend negative feelings, and we open the heart. We love ourselves more and believe in our abilities, and place a high value on our precious time and talents. When we are highly esteemed, we can begin making decisions based on what inspires us. This is how we become highly accomplished and successful.

And so, follow the whispers of your heart, make decisions based on what inspires you and create a joyful existence, and therefore you inspire others to do the same. It's catchy! And everyone wins.

Fear drowns imagination.

Give These a Whirl:

1. *Write a list of your 10 best attributes (strengths). Then list 10 attributes you think are weaknesses. Now determine how each of them, strengths and weaknesses, benefit you in achieving your creative dream. Turn the weaknesses into strengths and you have a balanced perspective. It also gives you more energy to pursue your passions.*

2. *Experiment with music while you are working on a creative project, whether you are planning, developing ideas, writing or drawing. Be in tune with how it impacts your feelings, thoughts and energy level. Try a variety of music genres such as classical, jazz, rock and roll, R&B, pop and country. Dust*

83

off your old albums stuffed away in milk crates and give them a spin. How do the various types of music impact you and your creative work? Experiment with music over the course of a day, evening or weekend, or longer.

3. *Make a list of all the important or influential people around you. It does not matter whether you like or dislike them. It could be a boss, parent, business partner, mentor, in-law. For each person write down what you have learned from them or how they have helped guide you. Spend a few moments absorbing what they have taught you. Be grateful for having these teachers around. Above all, send them good thoughts.*

4. *Write a list of everything you are grateful for. It could be your loved ones, a joyful experience, talents, a pet, a child, a house, education, job, income sources, an automobile, travel experiences, good health, beauty, wisdom, a hobby, etc. Keep going until you have exhausted everything you are truly grateful for. Spend hours if you must.*

Fire-Breathing Dragons, Energy Vampires, Challengers and Champions

Teachers open the door, but you must enter by yourself.
-- Chinese proverb

Who are the people you surround yourself with? Your friends, family, colleagues, lovers. How do you describe them? How do they make you feel when in their presence? Do they support you and your ideas? Or do they criticize your imagination and intentions? Do they cheer you on? Or do they think you are crackers?

We must have an honest, realistic perspective of the people we surround ourselves with. "Birds of a feather, flock together," to borrow from the old adage. Sometimes we have to rewire our thinking regarding the way we perceive other people and how they impact our feelings, spirit, imagination and productivity.

For those people who impact us negatively, taking the extreme measure of letting them go may be a difficult, but necessary, course of action. Ultimately, it is best to love them by being non-judgemental and wishing them well, while limiting your exposure to them.

If you aim to unlock your creative power and turn your dreams into reality, there are certain personalities that you should become aware of and how they impact you.

The Fire-Breathing Dragon:

Negative thinkers destroy our creative ability, our imagination and our dreams. These negative thinkers are *Fire-Breathing Dragons* and they sizzle your creative juices before you can say hogwash. A *Fire-Breathing Dragon* is full of doom and gloom, pooh-poohing ideas, constantly expressing reasons why an idea or initiative should *not* work.

One of my favourite examples of a negative character is Eeyore from the classic children's story, *Winnie the Pooh*, whose gloomy demeanour is as heavy as the bear's honey is thick. I am not sure how you feel, but I certainly did not want to spend too much time hanging out with Eeyore.

Fire-Breathing Dragons do not serve our creative minds by breathing their negative breath on us. Take a look at the people around you and determine if there is a negative thinking *Fire-Breathing Dragon* amongst them. Be honest, because denial does not serve you here. Negative people get too much out of being negative; that is why they are negative. As difficult as it may seem, you are better off without their draining energy.

I find the best way of handling a *Fire-Breathing Dragon* is to do a "time out." In a loving and kind manner, let them know you are submerged in a creative project and need time and space to pursue it. If they sincerely care about you, they will understand. This may be difficult to do with colleagues in a workplace environment, but if you are feeling negatively impacted by someone in your place of work perhaps a change of employment is the better route to go.

The Energy Vampire:

Besides the negative thinker, there is the *Energy Vampire* – an equally negative force creative people are advised to keep at arm's length. The *Energy Vampire* is someone who drains you of energy whenever you are in their company. You feel exhausted after even the briefest of visits. An *Energy Vampire* is highly selfish, because they are drowning in their own pain and lack of inspiration and creativity. The *Energy Vampire* enjoys drawing people into their melodrama, and gives little regard or consideration to others. In other words, it is a one-way relationship.

One of my former neighbours was an energy vampire. She talked non-stop about what was going on in her life and rarely did she ask me about mine. Whenever I was in her presence, I felt exhausted to the point I simply avoided contact as much as possible, although it was difficult considering we lived so close to each other. But I had to limit communication to give myself the time and space I required to keep my own energy for the sake of my creative projects.

We are not doing ourselves any service by having highly selfish *Energy Vampires* in our lives. They suck creativity out of your blood. It does not mean we do not love them, but, again, it is better to love them by being non-judgemental and wishing them well, without necessarily having to expose yourself to them.

The Challenger:

Having a friend, family member, colleague or boss who challenges us is a different story. Someone who challenges us stimulates our creative mind, passion and inspiration, and usually has our best interest at heart. Constructive criticism – it must be *constructive* -- is valuable for supporting us and challenging us to grow. *The Challenger* is just that: someone who challenges us to grow and reach our creative heights. In fact, it is an excellent idea to find a mentor or several mentors who challenge you.

Keep in mind a *Challenger* may tells us things we do not want to hear. For instance, they may feel we are making a mistake (in other words, having a life lesson), or question our intentions. They may wonder if the decisions we make are best for us. Do not view this as negativity. They most likely have your best interest at heart. Take into consideration the advice a *Challenger* gives you. Listen to what they have to say without judging them. You can choose to dismiss their advice, but they probably have an invaluable message to offer, from the heart.

The Champion:

The *Champion* is our best ally. A *Champion* gets squarely behind us, pushing us along our path. The *Champion* is a supporter and cheerleader. The *Champion* is also our safety net when things go awry, allowing us to fall back with our eyes closed into their trusted, loving arms. It is highly beneficial to surround yourself with lots and lots of people who support you.

In summary, it is very difficult to be highly creative with people who have negative energy hanging around us because they deplete our own energy sources. Therefore, it is best to love them and be non-judgemental, while limiting your exposure to them (be sure to send them good thoughts). Conversely, say "hello" with a smiling open heart to *Challengers* and *Champions*, and to people who are inspiring to you. They give you energy and inspiration to keep you tucking along the path you are designed to follow.

Give This a Whirl:

Write out a list of the people you associate with from the moment you wake up to the time you tuck yourself into bed. Against each name, write down one word that sums up their personality, and whether they have a positive or negative impact on you. Identify the Challengers and Champions and put big stars against their names. By doing this exercise you gain valuable perspective. Revisit this list now and again to refresh your mind.

Use Your Whole Brain

Worse than being blind is to see and have no vision.
-- Helen Keller

Researchers suggest we use two different styles of thinking – analytical and creative -- controlled by two different hemispheres of the brain, the left brain and the right brain. Each of us tends to have a preference or dominance. For example, studies have shown that lawyers, engineers and bankers tend to be predominately left brained. Writers, artists, musicians and entrepreneurs (think of the dotcom gurus of the '90s) tend to be predominately right brained.

Left Brain	Right Brain
Analytical	Holistic
Logical	Intuitive
Verbal	Pictoral
Sequential	Simultaneous
Temporal	Spatial

Like it or not, we live in a society that values analytical, linear thinking; one of logic, conformity and order. From the time you were a young child you have learned this (directly or indirectly) from parents, teachers, older siblings, grandparents; and other influential role models such as Girl Guide leaders, soccer coaches, and so on. Therefore, you probably grew up undervaluing your creative thinking side; that of the arts, aesthetics, feeling and imagination.

A dear friend of mine is an executive in a major corporation, but what he really wants to do is write a novel. He has great ideas for stories, but to-date he has not started his project. I once asked him why he does not "just begin," he told me he does not feel he is creative enough. This is hard to believe because he is bright, articulate and has fascinating ideas; therefore I am certain he could find a way to express himself using the written word. So, I probed some more. Like many of us he grew up in a family that does not value creativity. His family encouraged him to concentrate his studies in "math and science," and to seek out a vocation based on logic and analytical thinking...none of this "frivolous artsy-fartsy stuff." So, he found his way to a field that, alas, demands strong analytical thinking. He is definitely good at what he does, but that is beside the point. My friend has all the "tools" to write a book, and be successful at it, but believes he does not have a creative bone in his body. Yet he has great ideas.

Like me, perhaps you began printing with your left hand, but your first teacher, one of the most influential people in your childhood, made you switch to the right – to conform. Or maybe you wanted to go to drama school, but your parents forbade it because they were concerned about how you would "pay the bills" once you were on your own. Or perhaps you did not have the confidence in yourself in art class to create what you desired, but it did not matter anyway because you were told you should "focus on math and science," and view art as recreational and frivolous.

Now it is time to get *rewired*.

There are benefits to having a society that values analytical thinking. If we were all using *only* our creative side (right brain), there would be no logic, orderliness or analyzing. We would *not* have medicine, technological advancements, a legal system, roads, law enforcement or financial advisors and other people to take care of our money or run our businesses. If we only used our creative side, everyone would have their heads in the dreamy clouds of imagination, and oh what a colourful world it would be.

However, if we as a society *only* used our analytical side (left brain), life would be very, very boring. We would *not* have music, art, books, movies, sitcoms, cartoon characters, comics, animation, architecture, graphic design and so forth. We would all conform and be the same.

It is ideal to have a balance of creative *and* analytical thinking, and there is more benefit to valuing *both*. *Whole brain* thinking uses both the analytical and the creative sides equally well, accessing both sides of the brain's hemisphere at the same time. *A whole brain thinker is a creative genius who can also utilize his/her analytical side to plan out a way of earning a living from their ideas and dreams.* A person who uses both sides of their brain can efficiently blend creativity *and* business, and be highly successful.

Left Brain 'Analytical' Thinking	**Right Brain 'Creative' Thinking**
Connected to use of *right* hand	**Connected to use of *left* hand**
(to strengthen: use right hand as much as possible)	**(to strengthen: use left hand as much as possible)**

*One of the advantages of being disorderly is
that one is constantly making exciting discoveries.
-- A.A. Milne*

To Develop Whole Braining Thinking, Try These:

1. *Using a computer is a good example of a tool that allows people to expand their whole brain thinking. With both hands tapping away on the keyboard simultaneously, both hemispheres of the brain become strengthened with use (left hand connected to the creative right brain, right hand connected to the analytical left brain). Like any other muscle in the body, by working that muscle you develop it. Therefore, if you want to develop strong whole brain thinking, use a computer as much as possible.*

2. *Playing the piano is another great way to develop whole brain thinking, as is virtually any other musical instrument. It can also be relaxing and inspirational at the same time.*

Be Colourful

With an apple I will astonish Paris.
-- Paul Cézanne

Colour has been used and researched by humans for more than 2,000 years. Different cultures throughout the centuries were known to have experimented with colour, including the ancient Egyptians, Chinese, Aztecs and Greeks. From clothing to architecture to spiritual healing to scientific studies, colour has played an important role in our culture and evolution.

Let's explore the colour *red* and its impact on our culture.

Historically, obtaining pure bright colours from dyes, which were derived from natural sources, was extremely labour intensive. Once technology enabled early society to process a highly desirable bright red colour, *red* became civilization's symbol of power.

In medieval times, people of power such as the nobility, kings, judges and executioners wore red robes or coats. Later, armies used the colour red for uniforms (today, the Royal Canadian Mounted Police dons red). Red has been used in the political arena (e.g. a symbol of communism and socialism). Many corporations today use red in their logos and identity for impact and recognition (test yourself…name one corporation that uses red). Products are draped with red labels or packaging to stand out on shelves. Red is used to warn us of danger on the roads, yet is also a fashionable colour for sports cars. Red is the colour of blood. Not quite as obvious, but very important, infrared radiation is used as a healing tool in medicine.

It is a well-known fact that colour has a vital impact on our moods, well-being and productivity. According to scientists, seeing colour affects us in body, mind and spirit. The human eye can see a wide-range of colours, with some colours or various combinations bringing about profound reactions. Some colours are eyesores (bright yellow). Others are soothing (baby pink), or can minimize fatigue (pastel blue), and promote balancing and healing (green, blue). Some are depressing (black, grey). Historically, some colours have been known to promote fertility (green).

Everything on earth is made of electromagnetic energy vibrating at different frequencies that correspond to sound, light and colour. We view our reality through sound, light and colour frequencies. Colour is actually light made of different frequencies and wavelengths; each colour has its own frequency and wavelength (the primary colours are what we know as the "rainbow" spectrum). There is no doubt we live in a world where colour dominates our lives, from seeing traffic signs, to noting weather patterns in the sky, to identifying food, to identifying people of different races.

Colour can be used by therapists to correct imbalances in the body and promote harmony with the body's own vibrations.

The colours we use in our workplace and home environments create ambience and impacts mood and creative energy. Colours can be used in a variety of combinations to get different effects. Many hospitals and health centres choose the soft colours of pink or blue or even pure white for the walls to get a particular effect. Corporations often use boring or dull colours like grey, white and brown. The next time you walk into a house that feels "warm and homey," check out the colour scheme the owner used.

As far as clothing is concerned, the colours you choose *to wear* may enhance or depress your creativity. The colours you wear are believed to send signals to others around you and each colour is associated with different personality characteristics. If you want to feel more cheerful, wear cheerful colours such as y*ellow.* If you want to feel sophisticated and powerful, wear *black,* a colour traditionally worn by artists. Black can also be used to create more space for reflection and inner searching, and can enhance another colour's energy when used in combination. *Red* is energizing, passionate, courageous and often reserved for extroverts. *Pink* is soft and approachable, and mostly viewed as feminine. *Indigo* is inspiring and traditional. *Blue* is honest and logical; it is also calming, relaxing and healing. *Orange* is sporty and outgoing; it can also stimulate creativity. *Brown* is conservative and down-to-earth. *White* is pure and neutral. *Violet* is calming for the body and mind.

Even the colour of food can impact our daily lives. Children, for instance, love anything colourful, which is the reason marketers have launched products such as multi-coloured cereals, green ketchup and blue French fries, to appeal to this market and create excitement.

If you want to be more creative, begin to see and experience this world in colour.

Did you know...

- *I spy with my little eye something that is...turquoise, no, beige! That is the colour of the Universe – beige -- according to scientists at John Hopkins University. However, when the scientists first announced the Universe's colour based on their research, it was claimed to be turquoise. Shortly thereafter, they admitted they made a mistake and concluded the colour of the Universe is actually boring beige.*

- *Red-headed women were once believed to be witches or whores.*

- *Only half of the denim in "blue jeans" is actually dyed blue. The other half is comprised of white weft threads. They could just as easily be called "white jeans."*

- *Roman Emperors wore purple robes.*

- *The poppy was once known as the devil's flower.*

- *Blue was once the colour of fidelity. Blue flowers such as forget-me-nots and violets symbolize faithfulness.*

- *In 1862, the United State's paper currency was created to help pay for the Civil War. The paper notes were printed the colour green and redeemable for coins "on demand." Hence, the name "greenback."*

There is logic of colours, and it is with this alone,
and not with the logic of the brain,
that the painter should conform.
-- Paul Cézanne

Try This:

Check out your wardrobe, your walls, furniture, art, even the food
you eat. Experiment with colour. Pay attention to colour around you.
Use it to the best of your ability. See how it impacts your energy level,
productivity and creative thinking.

Give Your Life a Shake!

Einstein once said we would never solve the problems of the world from the level of thinking we were at when we created them.

Challenge Rules and Embrace Change

Everywhere we turn there are rules for this and that. Schools have rules. Corporations have rules. Countries have rules. Institutions have rules, as do restaurants and stores. Families have rules. Even you have your own rules. Rules are everywhere. *Challenge the rules.* Rules are to be followed; yet they are also meant to be broken -- it leads to change. Change is valuable: it is evolution. As a creative person, it is valuable to *challenge the rules.* In a way, it is our duty to society.

By all means, I am not suggesting people must go out and commit wrongful acts or disobey laws. What I am referring to are the unwritten or informal societal rules, or self-imposed rules, such as rules of conduct and ways of thinking.

Creative thinking is about constantly challenging the rules. One of the 20th Century's greatest artists, Pablo Picasso, provides us with pervading insight: "Every act of creation is also an act of destruction." The act of creation is first and foremost an act of destruction. Creation demands *duality*, therefore you must be willing to destroy in order to build up. Moreover, creative thinking is not only about generating new ideas and concepts. It is about *transcending* old ideas, concepts and beliefs, too. Only by breaking away from conventional thinking can we generate new ideas and approaches. Consider this for a moment: if we did not challenge rules, society would never evolve. If society had not evolved, you would not be reading these words on this page today. This is the reason why challenging rules is so valuable.

Many moons ago, before the concept of casual Friday's took off, I worked at a prestigious agency where everyone wore conservative business suits every day. It was not a written rule, it was just so. To me, the dress code did not always make sense, because as a public relations firm we were expected to be progressive and creative. That was the reason clients hired us. Except, I kept wondering to myself: "How can

I possibly come up with hot ideas if I am wrapped in uncomfortable armour all day?" So, one day I broke the dress code, albeit nervously, and wore comfy jeans so I could feel unrestricted enough to do my best creative work. Eyebrows raised, but no one said a word. A few days later, I appeared in jeans again. Still, raised eyebrows, but not one senior executive scolded me. So, I did it again. Soon thereafter, a colleague wore jeans. Then another staff member, then another...until eventually we turned into a more casual and comfortable place to do creative work, at least for some people.

My point is not that one must wear jeans to be creative. Rather, one must be willing and courageous enough to challenge the rules in order to make changes.

Generally speaking *change is good*. Change is a Universal law that happens whether we embrace it, or resist it. As recording artist Carly Simon so wisely sings, "I know nothing stays the same." In order to reach new creative heights, we must be willing to try new things, different approaches and ways of thinking. We must be open to new possibilities. If you open yourself up to change and transformation, your creativity opens up as well.

Mix Up Routine

Routine has its comforts, it feels safe and secure, but it can become terribly boring. It is predictable. It is about avoiding going into the unknown. Let's face it, routine is complacency and it is not necessarily a friend of the creative mind.

If you mix up your regular routine, you will probably feel refreshed and stimulated. Whenever you feel blue, creatively stuck or going nowhere fast with your projects, do an enjoyable activity or something different to mix it up. There are times when you might want to mix up your routine for the heck of it. If you feel creatively drained try something you would not normally do. Have a real hoot! For instance, why not skip work for the afternoon to catch a flick, hit a beach or share some screams with a friend at an amusement park? Get yourself a motorcycle or a skateboard if you want. Take up ballroom dancing or snowboarding. Why not?

An excellent way of mixing up that ho-hum routine is to *travel*. Travel is relaxing and stimulating. It can also be adventurous and exhilarating. Pack a bag, or backpack, and go somewhere -- anywhere -- whether it is a day trip, a weekend get-away or longer. Chances are whenever you return from a trip you find that you are ready and willing to make all sorts of changes in routine that stimulates you. It does not have to be an expensive trip either. If budget is an issue, spend the day exploring an unfamiliar neighbourhood, on foot if need be. Or have a picnic at a nearby lake or park. Some days I simply walk a different route with my dog. By doing this I find that I rediscover my own neighbourhood. I also enjoy taking Sunday drives to nearby scenic towns or villages and dashing into the shops.

There is one other thing I wish to mention about routine. Have you ever counted how many times each day you pick up the telephone, send an e-mail or answer a page? Have you ever logged how much time it takes out of your day to do so? In order to fully tap into your creative juices, it is truly beneficial to *tune out* now and again from the daily drone of telecommunication. We get into the habit of needlessly being "on call," which is often nothing more than a distraction for our creativity. When working on a project, or simply to rejuvenate your spirit, consider turning off the phone, not answering e-mails and shutting off the pager. One day a week I let my computer sleep; it needs its rest, too. One day a week is not much to ask.

Shake It Up with Laughter!

Laughter is terrific medicine for the creative mind and a great way to give our spirits a vitality shake. Humans love to laugh; it makes us feel good. The average adult laughs 17 times per day. Laughter makes us healthier and happier. Embrace humour and give your belly a hardy shake.

When times are challenging and energy is negative, reading the comics or a joke book can be just the medicine the creative doctor ordered. Or call a friend who has a wicked sense of humour. Relish in your own style of humour and develop a knack for telling jokes: this uses your creativity. Tune into a sitcom on television for a chuckle once in a while, or better yet, check out a live comedy act. Shake up your creative spirit with laughter.

What is the difference between Laughter vs Humour?

- *Laughter is not the same thing as humour. Laughter is the physiological reaction to something we find humorous.*

- *Laughter comprises of two actions working together: body gestures and the making of a sound (and I do not mean gas).*

How to Have More Laughter Every Day:

- *Discover what makes you laugh and do it as much as possible.*

- *Hang out with funny people more often.*

- *Develop your own style of humour, whether it is telling jokes or a writing style.*

- *Take a comedy class. Not only does it help one find humour, it boosts self-confidence.*

- *Read the morning comics.*

- *Find the humour in difficult circumstances. If you look hard enough, you will find it.*

Open Your Mind to Other Ways of Living and Doing Things

A closed mind means closed opportunities. An open mind looks at different ways of living and doing everyday things. There are times when a change of lifestyle may be more suitable for our creative needs. Maybe we must consider selling assets so we can survive off the proceeds in order to launch a new business. Maybe buying a houseboat sounds grand, just because it is a dream we have always had, or maybe it makes economical sense.

In life, we are constantly in transition and change; nothing on planet earth is permanent. Permanency is nothing more than an illusion. Therefore we might as well make changes that allow us to follow ours dreams. Think *positive transformation*. If we are not proactive in making the necessary changes in our lives, the Universe makes them for us. I know that I am much more willing and able to make a change when it is my choice, rather than it being forced upon me. Nothing stays the same, therefore we are better off opening our minds to other ways of living and doing things, even if we have to roll with the punches.

Be Spontaneous and Flexible

While rigidity can be beneficial under certain circumstances, too much rigidity may trap the creative mind, such as sticking to regimented routine or following rules "come hell or high water." There are times to follow rules, there are times to question them, and there are times to break them. If we are being rigid in our thinking, we are not open-minded and therefore have no room for spontaneity. *Many of our new ideas or concepts are born from spontaneous insights.* As far as creativity is concerned, living by extremes and absolutes is taxing. It can back us into corners and limit our potential.

Consider for a moment the military, in general, as an example of rigid thinking at the extreme end of the spectrum. The military is not exactly known to foster independent, creative thinking from its soldiers. Rather, it wants one unified entity that works toward one common cause (e.g. homeland protection). While this undoubtedly has its value and benefits, I use it here as an example to provide a point of comparison of how rigid our thinking can be.

For your creativity's sake, it is wise to be spontaneous and flexible whenever it makes sense -- not as a rule, but as a way of life -- and therefore you will find your creativity blossoming.

100

Identify and Overcome Unwanted Patterns

Unwanted patterns use up energy and hold us back from being creative. Whether they are negative thoughts (e.g. I am not good enough) or more obvious self-sabotaging tendencies (e.g. substance abuse), it serves us well to identify unwanted patterns and strive to overcome them. Often these patterns are subtle, such as reaching for the cookie jar when we are upset, or being hooked on searching for the wrong guy or girl. Attracting emotional disasters is another example. So is wasting money like it was toilet paper. Or wasting precious time, for that matter.

Unwanted patterns may be difficult for us to overcome without professional help. Under these circumstances it is good for our creativity and general well-being to source it out. When we do, we also get a bonus: by overcoming unwanted patterns, we increase our self-worth. We also become more creative.

One pattern many people engage in is watching a lot of television. After a long day's work, they get into a pattern of flopping on a sofa, turning on the tube and surfing all night long. There are definitely some marvellous informational and entertaining programs on television. It can also be a super way of generating new ideas, finding humour and learning about inspiring people. However, it is important to determine when we are getting value from the experience, and when we are using it as a way to escape reality. Some escapism is fine on occasion (it can be quite pleasurable), and television definitely has a valuable place in this world. However, it is essential to be aware of where we are putting our precious time and energy. The more time we spend watching television, the more time it takes us away from creation. Bear in mind that time, once passed, is something we never, *ever* recover. Therefore it serves us well to use the gift of the time we have on this earth wisely.

Of course, the same thing applies to surfing the Internet.

Conversely, there are instances when certain patterns are *beneficial.* Getting into a pattern of saving money and managing it properly is highly beneficial. So is shopping for healthy food, eating greens, taking vitamins, exercising regularly and drinking oceans of water.

Creation demands duality.

101

I Dare You to Try These:

1. *Think of your daily routine. Write down your regular pattern: what you do from morning until night. What could you do differently to mix it up? Walk your dog on a different route? Drive a different way to work? Jog on a different path? Sleep in and work late? Have a siesta? Eat nothing but healthy foods? Changing your routine, even in small bites, is a valuable way to stimulate your creative spirit and get a refreshing take on life.*

2. *What if life began the moment you died, and the point of conception was actually your death? What would happen in all that time in between? How would your life play out? Envision what you might experience then write a few paragraphs or pages about it. I realize it sounds silly, but when you see how it plays out you may experience profound insights that get you thinking differently.*

3. *Write a list of the top 5 places in the world you long to visit. They do not have to be far from home if budget is tight. Think of places beyond your backyard where you can unwind and become inspired. Then devise an action plan to help you get to these places.*

4. *Identify unwanted patterns that use energy and take your heart away from your creative dreams. These patterns can include activities such as watching too much television, spending too much time surfing the Internet or reading a lot of novels that you do not even enjoy. Are you using these activities to escape painful emotions or circumstances? It is wise to make the necessary adjustments to change these patterns so you can have more energy to focus on creation. If you find yourself overwhelmed, it is good to find a caring, non-judgmental friend or a professional to talk to.*

Live With Courage, Take Risks

Try saying this mantra aloud to yourself: "Out of my zone of comfort lies my destiny." Now repeat it: "Out of my zone of comfort lies my destiny."...and again...

This is a terrific mantra to live by. It can help inspire you and get you out of a tight spot, especially when making decisions and taking big risks. Risk-taking is directly linked to our comfort zone. No risk, no reward! Stay safe, stay stuck. Repeating this mantra -- *out of my zone of comfort lies my destiny* -- is a good habit to get into, and not a habit to break.

Some people are better than others at risk-taking. Why? At its basic core, it comes down to having confidence -- or self-worth. Taking big risks is not for the faint of heart either. Think for a moment of some of the mega-rich icons or super-size celebrities in the world. They all have one thing in common: they take risks.

Have you ever said to yourself, "Gee, I'd like to (insert desire here), but I know I am not good at it." We have all said that to ourselves at least once. Except, how do you know if you are not good at something if you do not take a risk and try it out? You have to start somewhere. Stay safe, stay stuck. Challenge yourself. It is best to set small goals at first, eventually establish larger ones. See how far you can go. Shoot for the moon, but know that if you only get to the end of your street it is okay. What is important is to take the risk and feel proud that you did.

Creativity Requires Courage

In order to take risks, we must drum up the courage to do so. According to renowned psychologist and philosopher Erich Fromm, "Creativity requires the courage to let go of certainties." We must be willing to walk into the unknown.

What if Columbus had not sailed across the ocean blue because he could not drum up enough courage? What if Einstein did not have the courage to share his theories with the world? What if Edison did not have the courage to invent the light bulb? What if Mother Teresa did not have the courage for compassion? What if not one single person had the courage to stand up to Hitler?

Our thoughts have a way of becoming reality. Believe in yourself and your ideas, and you take more risks. Take more risks and you experience more joy, success and wealth. By believing in yourself and taking risks, others believe in you, too. Like financial lenders. Or the buyers of your products.

It is one thing to come up with ideas, but it takes courage to share those ideas or concepts with others. It also requires courage to take action steps toward making those ideas and concepts a reality. It is risky. What sets apart the ordinary person from the extraordinary person is this: *the ability to courageously take action steps on ideas and concepts* -- to bring them to life and make them a reality.

But in order to be courageous, we have to first *feel* courageous. Whenever I need a courage boost, I engage in a ritual that keeps me *reminding* myself to *feel* courageous and it helps me stay on track. When walking my dog in the mornings, I say to myself, "I live with courage." I repeat it until I embody it and feel courageous. Try it for yourself. See how it changes your life in a short time.

Keep in mind that self-doubt thoughts can clip the wings of courage. When this happens, *visualization techniques* help to overcome those thoughts. When this occurs (inevitably it will, as it does to all of us), visualize yourself as being a person with utmost courage. See yourself as a real go-getter. Visualize yourself as someone who decides to act upon his/her desires and accepts whatever challenge is given to him/her. Try the "courage mantra" every morning.

- *Think of one person, any person in the world, who epitomizes courage to you. Someone who oozes courage. What is it about them that you feel is courageous? What have they achieved? Why do you admire them so? Embody that same kind of courage for yourself.*

Some famous people who exemplify courage:

- Joan of Ark
- Napoleon
- Catherine The Great of Russia
- Aristotle
- Stephen Hawking
- Rembrandt
- Da Vinci
- Helen Keller
- Martin Luther King
- Charles Darwin
- Princess Diana
- Bill Clinton
- The Unknown Soldier

In order to be successful in life, we must take risks. If creativity is first and foremost an act of destruction, *we must risk destroying before we can build up*. It takes a lot of courage to destroy. Creativity, by nature, involves making changes and taking risks. If we are risk-aversive, our creative spirit flounders. If we are risk-aversive, we are also *unlucky in creativity*. Even in relationships we cannot achieve a successful union without taking the risk of opening up the heart and trusting the other person. If we become risk-aversive, we are unlucky in love. It is the same with our creative endeavours.

When we are feeling good about ourselves and are clear on our intentions, we take more risks. Keep this spiritual law in mind: *when your certainty is greater than your doubt, your certainty rules. When your certainty is greater than the doubt of someone else, you rule.* For instance, if you believe you can do something new that is out of your comfort zone, but others do not believe you can do it, you will rule because your certainty is greater than their doubt. Try it! Show them you can do it.

I remember the time I told my father I was considering moving abroad to work. I was only 21 years of age at the time and hell-bent on trying new things. As he sat in his chair reading the newspaper, my father's only response from behind his wall of ink was, coolly, "Shannon, you're such a dreamer." As if being a dreamer is *bad*...this got my back up. So, I thought to myself, *"Humph...I'll prove* to you just how much of a dreamer I am...watch me!" Next thing I knew I had purchased an airline ticket to England. I didn't just want to be a dreamer, but I wanted to prove that I could make it happen and move to another country all by myself. And so, my certainty that I could do it was far greater than my father's doubt and therefore I ruled -- and off to England I went. Unbeknownst to my father, *that* incident gave me the drive and courage that got my dreams rolling for years to come.

As we know, there are *pros* and *cons* to everything in life, and there is no exception with it comes to taking big risks. It is important to weigh the pros and cons of taking big risks. If you are unsure of taking a big risk, like changing careers or publishing a personal story that could hurt other people, you may want to consider writing down all the *benefits* that will come out of it, as well as all the *drawbacks*. This helps to get a complete picture. Once you weigh the pros and cons, and get a balanced perspective, you may decide it is a risk not worth taking. And that is okay.

If you have an important decision to make and get stuck or become afraid of moving forward, say to yourself: Who cares? Or...so what? Or...why not? Not to sound callous, but when you do not give a damn about what others think you are able to grow wings. You take risks. Your creativity flourishes. You no longer take *no* for an answer. You can persevere.

To be a successful risk-taker, keep focused on the reward for this helps to stay on track. There will be times when obstacles arise between you and your goals, but it is best to see them as challenges and keep in mind the desired outcome. Persevere.

At the end of the day, what are you willing to risk to live your creative dream? Or experience joy? What is the worst that could happen? Why not experience life to the fullest each and every day? What's to lose?

Live with courage. Take risks.

Out of your zone of comfort lies your destiny.

Give These a Whirl:

1. *Think of a big risk you would like to take, but have not been able to drum up the courage to do so (in business, relationship, finances). Write out a list of benefits (pros) of taking the risk. Then write out the drawbacks (cons) of taking the risk. On a separate sheet of paper, write out all the drawbacks to you if you do not take the risk. Get a complete picture and a balanced perspective, and you will be willing and able to take more risks.*

2. *Never say "never"... What is the craziest activity that you always said you would never do (i.e. rock climbing, take flying lessons, scuba-dive, ask a celebrity on a date, publish a story about your personal life, paint a nude portrait)? How would it change you if you actually did it? Envision it and then write a paragraph or two about the experience. "Never" is an absolute and it is wise to use it sparingly when it comes to creative thinking.*

3. *Make a list of all the significant risks you took throughout your adult years. In each case, how did you benefit from the outcome? How did each outcome, positive or negative, help you get to where your heart desires to go? For example, you may discover that a financial setback forced you to become more creative.*

It's All a Learning Experience

Do not fear mistakes – there are none.
-- Miles Davis

There is no such thing as a *mistake*. There are only *lessons*.

By taking this perspective it eliminates much of the fear of trying something new or different. It is all about perspective. Really it is.

It is usually the fear of making a mistake that holds us back from taking bold steps forward. Often that F-word, *fear*, is associated with an event that happened in the past, such as a bad relationship, sour business deal or harsh criticism, and we project the possible feared outcome (an illusion) in the future. However, every time we take steps forward in our evolution, steps toward our dreams, we have much to gain by the experience alone.

Learn Your Lessons

When it comes to something new, try and try again; but we must learn from our lessons. If it does not work out, strive to learn from it. *We do not evolve until we learn our lessons.* Whenever we do not learn a lesson, the Universe presents the same lesson to us again and again and again until we learn it. How many people do you know who keep repeating lessons unlearned, such as finding themselves in one relationship after another that is not good for them, or recklessly spending their way into deep debt? These people keep getting the same lessons and, since they do not learn from them, the pattern continues until the day they learn the lesson. It is the same with our creative minds.

When we learn our lessons, we evolve.

Many years ago, I got involved in a project that was once part of my dream. I did not do my homework and, as a result, it cost me more money than anticipated. This taught me lessons that have prepared me for even bigger lessons. I learned how *not* to run a business. I learned how *not* to treat people in business. I learned the value of being with people with vision. I also learned that you should never trust anyone else with your money: a crucial lesson, and a humbling one at that. If I had looked at the experience as a mistake, that perspective would not have given me the wisdom I gained from seeing it as a lesson, which probably prevented me from losing a larger sum of money.

Overcome Obstacles

The fear of making a mistake is an *obstacle in your mind*. We are best served to identify the obstacles in the way of achieving our dreams and do what it takes to overcome them. Not only does this take us closer to our goals, we also increase our self-worth. Obstacles are meant to show us what we have not yet learned. They are simply challenges.

Overcome obstacles and learn the lessons. When we learn our lessons, we are no longer presented with the same obstacles. As well, every time we overcome obstacles, we feel more powerful, increase our creativity and our potential to accomplish greater feats in this world.

Persistence is key to moving forward with ideas and projects, and overcoming those obstacles. Do not get stuck in la-la land. Do not give up. Rather, be persistent. Walt Disney had a heck of a time selling his concept for a theme park, yet he persisted. He believed in his idea, persevered and was willing to "make mistakes" because he saw the value in lessons. Lucielle Ball persisted until she reached her dream of being an actress, and because of her tenacity she became one of the most beloved comic actresses in history. In her autobiography *Love, Lucy,* the late diva of comedy wrote with great wisdom about the valuable learning from the "perceived" misgivings she experienced.

Writers constantly face the fear of making mistakes, or of failure, which often leads to the proverbial writer's block. It is a well-understood fact that writers receive more rejections than acceptances for their work. Some have been known to wallpaper rooms with rejection letters. If a writer stopped at the first "no thank you," with a heart broken into pieces, they would never get their work published or made into films or plays. Eventually, hopefully, someone will say "yes." The writer will never know unless they continue to engage in the rules of the game. Imagine if writers like Hemmingway, J.K. Rowling and Tolkien did not share their work with the world for fear of making a mistake, or of failure, we would not be enjoying their beautiful stories today. The same concept applies to anyone who is selling an idea or a program or a widget. What is important is to not give up. Be persistent.

If seemingly insurmountable obstacles arise causing us to freeze in our tracks, we begin asking ourselves whether to proceed with our dreams. For as long as your project is in your heart, keep going forward. Persist until you absolutely know going forward is futile. You cannot lose. You can only gain from the experience. Why? Because there are no mistakes, only valuable lessons. It is all a learning experience.

Trust the Creative Process

While it may not come easy, it is important to trust the creative process. In a way, trusting the process *is* part of the creative process. Transcending the fear of making a mistake and getting beyond self-doubt is part of that process. So is learning to *enjoy* the process. While you are at it, adopt the attitude: what will be, will be. Ideas are like seeds planted in the ground: some ideas grow, others may not. Some projects get completed, others may not. Some projects are critically acclaimed, others are slammed by the critics. No matter what the end result is, there is much to learn from the experience of the creative process itself.

There are no mistakes, only valuable lessons. It is all a learning experience. What is important is to learn our lessons and move on. This is the way we evolve as humans. Take this perspective: when you see the positive in a crisis, there is no problem.

Whenever an idea or project fails, pull up your socks, learn from it and either try again or let it go if that is the wiser course of action. The key is to believe in yourself. *Everything is perspective.* We can choose to make a mistake and live with regret and resentment or fear of it being repeated, or we can choose to see a mistake as a lesson and learn from it, and gain some valuable wisdom. The choice is ours, and ours alone.

Edison tried 9,000 experiments to perfect the light bulb. That's 8,999 lessons before he got it right.

Give These a Whirl:

1. *List five of what you believe are your biggest failures. Now list what you learned from each failure. How have your perceived failures actually helped you get what you desire? For example, perhaps you feel you failed at making a new business a success. But you discover that you learned new skills and talents during that experience. How have these new skills and talents actually helped you get where your heart yearns to go now?*

2. *What is the biggest fear that stands in the way of creating your dream? How would you benefit by tackling that fear? Where would it take you? How would it make you feel? What would you learn? Write a few paragraphs about how you see the experience unfolding.*

Ask Quality Questions

Ask a different question and the marvellous answer appears.
-- Rumi

My mentor once said to me these wise words that forever changed me: "The quality of your questions determines the quality of your life. If you want a good quality of life, ask yourself good quality questions."

If you want to be all you can be creatively, ask yourself lots and lots of quality questions. In return, you will receive the gifts of valuable insight, clarity and guidance.

It is said that Sir Isaac Newton discovered gravity when he observed an apple falling to the ground from its branch at the *same time* as he noticed the moon hanging in the sky. He asked himself, "Why did the apple fall, and yet why does the moon *not* fall? And does the same law that caused the apple to fall also apply to the moon?" It was undoubtedly a significant question that revolutionized science and the way we perceive or understand Universal laws, but was it a *general* question, or was it a *quality* question?

What is a *quality question* and how is it different than a *general question*, you ask? *Quality questions are those aligned with the values of one's heart.* In other words, they are based on what is truly in your heart. And the more specific the question, the better. If we are not willing to ask ourselves quality questions, we can remain frozen in time. We go nowhere fast. Asking quality questions gets us thinking differently, even radically. It motivates us. It expands our boundaries and horizons. It gets us excited about opportunities. It can be liberating. Asking quality questions helps us zero in on solutions that enable us to transform what is an "okay" life to a really great one. *A creative mind is a curious mind.* Asking quality questions helps us gain wisdom and perspective, our creativity is stimulated and we can reach new heights and impact more people in positive or profound ways.

Here is an example of a question many of us have asked ourselves at least once: "How can I make ends meet?" This is a rather general question. If I change the emphasis according to the values of my heart and be more specific, bearing in mind each of us has personalized values unique to us, I can turn it into a quality question: "How can I make <u>more money now than ever</u> using my <u>creative talents</u>?"

Humm…how can I make MORE money now than ever using my creative TALENTS? So you see the subtle difference in the emphasis? That subtle difference can mean the difference between a dollar and a million bucks. By asking quality questions you can really give yourself quality answers in tune with your heart. You can start making decisions and taking action toward what you love. Your passion flares up and propels you forward.

If you ask quality questions you get quality answers and ultimately lead a good quality life. You come up with quality ideas, quality projects, quality business ventures, quality jobs. You have more quality friends. As well, ask quality people quality questions. That is, ask those people who have mastered their desires questions that are aligned with the values of your heart. The wisdom these masters impart will most certainly help guide you.

If you feel you have made a "mistake" (read: having a life lesson) or are presented with a challenge, a quality question to try is: "How is this (insert: idea, problem, situation) helping me achieve my deepest desire?" By asking yourself this quality question you gain wisdom and perspective, which inevitably helps to expand your creativity.

Other examples of quality questions to try are:

- *How can this setback help me reach my goal?*

- *How can I turn this negative situation into something positive?*

- *How can I get all the "gifts" I want?*

- *How can my quirks best serve my creativity?*

- *How can I get more energy to accomplish my creative desires?*

- *What are the steps I need to make to move myself from a*

student to a master?

- *What is holding me back from manifesting my creative desires, and what do I need to do to change that?*

In order to ask ourselves quality questions, questions aligned with the values of our heart, *we must be fully aware of what those values are.* We must first know with certainty and clarity who we are and what our purpose in life is, and therefore what our values are. It would be highly beneficial to do a little exploration of your heart and soul if you are unsure what your true values are.

As well, I encourage you to ask other people questions about their creative projects. It will keep them inspired and will, in return, inspire you. You may even experience a new twist of fate in your own life with something you learned or discovered, just by asking them questions and showing interest.

Quality questions are in-line with your values and what your heart is whispering to you. Quality questions are specific. The more specific the better. Ask your inner guide specific questions that stimulate your imagination and keep you growing toward what you desire.

What If?...

Another way of stimulating our creative thinking is to ask ourselves questions that are based on the hypothetical notion: *"What If?"* For instance, "What If"... I actually finished writing my book? "What If"... the sun never set? "What if"... Newton's apple rotted on the branch instead of falling on the ground? "What if"...the telephone was never invented? "What if"... I was famous? "What if"... dogs walked people? "What If"... we all had a twin living on the planet? "What if"...I had no fear?

As you are mulling over or exploring ideas or concepts, or need to make a decision, ask yourself "What If?" questions. It stimulates the imagination and expands our limits. It also works great for problem-solving in business situations, or even in relationship conflict. Asking What If? questions helps us wrap our minds around the issue, enabling solutions to present themselves.

114

Stephen King claims to ask himself What If? questions when developing his ideas, something he feels is significant.

I personally enjoy the process of deconstructing philosophical theories about the Universe, spirituality, religion and humanity, and asking lots of "What If?" questions about these theories. If we all believed what we were told, we would still be living in the dark. We would not have the printing press, computer, automobile, airplane, telephone, television or film. When you look at it this way, it is vital that we ask questions – of ourselves and of others.

Ask quality questions. Ask hypothetical "What If?" questions. What is important is to consistently ask questions. A creative mind is a curious mind by nature. So give yourself the freedom to be curious and inquisitive. Children, for instance, are notoriously curious, which is one reason they are also highly imaginative. We all have that inner child within us until the day we pass away. Therefore we should all honour our child-like quality for it continues to keep us inquisitive and imaginative.

As a creative mind, observe the life around you. Open your eyes wide to what you see. Open your ears to what you hear. Most of all open your heart. And ask quality questions.

The life which is not examined is not worth living.
-- Plato

What If...You Tried These?

1. *Think of your creative dream (project, idea). Ask yourself: "What if...I am able to make more money than ever by being more creative? How could I help inspire others by using my creative talents? How could I help others benefit and have better lives with the money I earn?*

2. *Think "What If" you had been born a decade earlier. What would your life have looked like? What would you have done? Tried? Seen? Experienced? Worn? Picture yourself. Of*

course, this depends on the decade you were born...What If you were a flower child? What If you lived through the depression? What If you watched man walk on the moon for the first time? What If Elvis Presley had been your hero? What If you were forced to sit at the back of the bus? What If you learned to do the Twist? Write a paragraph or two about it.

The Balancing Act: Seven Areas of Life

Catch the vigorous horse of your mind.
-- *Zen saying*

According to the principles of *Inward Bound*, there are seven areas of life that we put our time and energy into: **career, finance, mental, social, spiritual, family and physical.**
We constantly go in and out of the seven areas. With this in mind, it is important to be clear on how we utilize our time and energy, and where we waste it. When we become aware of this, we can make adjustments and commit both time and resources to pursue our creative desires, and experience a life filled with joy and fulfillment.

If I had a dollar for every time I have heard these words: "I don't have the time to do (insert blank)." The key to balancing our energy and doing what we love is to *make the time.* Create time and space for your desires, and balance it with relaxation and fun activities that are vital for your health and spirit. Balancing our time and energy in all seven areas of life is one of the *best* ways to keep the beat of the whispering heart strong.

What does a balanced life look like?

Jane, a graphic designer, has a well-balanced life. She works at a full-time job she enjoys, but knows when it is time to call it a day. She takes a few hours each week to keep her financial house in order, organize her savings and plan for the future. She spends time with her spouse and other family members in the evenings, on weekends and holidays. She manages to take breaks to do the things that nourish her spirit, such traveling to inspiring places around the world, spending time at her cottage and taking walks on the beach. She reads a variety of subjects that interest her and keep her stimulated. She puts energy into developing meaningful relationships with friends and connects with inspiring people so she can learn and grow. And she manages to spend the time necessary to be as healthy as possible by staying active and eating healthy foods.

Since Jane has managed to fully balance her life in all seven areas, she feels vibrant, invigorated and joyful. She embraces life, accomplishes goals and has the time to create new dreams. And her vibrancy has rubbed off on her loved ones and others within her circle.

The Seven Areas of Life:

1. Career
2. Finance
3. Mental
4. Social
5. Spiritual
6. Family
7. Physical

It is important to be aware that we may be infatuated with some areas because they feel pleasant to our senses, therefore wanting to spend most of our time in those areas. Or we may resent an area of life because it feels bad to our senses, therefore avoiding that area as much as possible, even completely. A healthy state is to have a *balance of all seven areas*.

For instance, someone who spends most of their time and energy working out may be doing it because it makes them feel good, or it boosts their ego. However, by spending most of their time in the physical area of life, they do not have much time for other areas -- such as family, for instance. Eventually, their family life or other areas such as finance or spiritual will suffer because they are spending most of their time working out.

Whereas someone who is not athletic may avoid taking care of their physical health because they loathe anything that means working their body. Instead they may be using their time and energy elsewhere -- to study at university, as an example. Instead of big biceps, they have big brains. Eventually, they will experience health problems since they are studying all the time and have not been taking care of their body, and they will be forced to slow down.

Or someone who works and manages their finances during most of their waking hours is so busy in the career and finance areas that they constantly cancel social engagements with friends. Eventually, the friends stop calling, and one day that person will wake up and realize they have no friends left.

None of these cases are ideal. Balance is best. When we do not have balance, the end result is that it takes us away from what we love, from our inspiration and from our creativity. We could all take a lesson from Jane.

It is wise to be aware of how you spend your time and energy, and strive to have balance. It makes your creative energy more productive in the long run. When we are busy creating something we love, we have more energy to do so. Although it takes energy to create, we feel more invigorated and joyful when we do. When we feel invigorated and joyful, we continue working on what we love and desire.

Creativity takes energy. Creativity can also give energy.

Balance Your Life With These:

Based on the Seven Areas of Life:

1. *One valuable exercise is to identify where you put your time and energy. First, list the activities you do on a regular basis in each of the seven areas. Then make a list of priorities of where you would LOVE to spend your energy – and stick to it. Your priorities may change from time to time, but become aware of the shifting pattern. Once the dust settles, check in with yourself and re-evaluate your priorities.*

2. *It is equally valuable to identify and write out all your core values (e.g. love, health, wealth, honesty, trust, reliability, etc.) and then prioritize them. Then you can make decisions aligned with your top values.*

3. *Another good exercise is to make a list of all the typical*

activities you do in one day (i.e. sleep, work, exercise, read, chores, etc.). For each activity, write down how much time it takes out of your day. Then see how much time these activities take over a course of one week. If you are able, create a pie chart with the data to give you a visual representation. Once you are finished, you will have perspective of where you put your time and how you might be able to be more balanced and energy-efficient.

After doing these exercises for the first time, you may discover that you waste precious time doing activities that are not serving your creativity.

Increase Vitality

To keep the body in good health is a duty...
otherwise we shall not be able to keep our mind strong and clear.
-- Buddha

Vitality is the body's state of being strong and active. It is pretty tough to be highly creative when we are stressed or not feeling well -- physically, mentally or spiritually. In order to be fully actualized creative beings, it is important to be in the best health possible and to focus our energy on what matters most to us. When we strive to maximize our vitality, it is easier to unleash our creative power.

What follows in this section are suggestions on ways to increase vitality to be more creative, and not to be considered as professional medical advice. Everyone is different. If you need to seek medical advice about your own personal health matters, please consult a physician.

Reduce Stress

To maximize our vitality, the first course of action is to take a *stress test*. If we determine we are stressed, we can then explore the factors that make us so stressed and then take the necessary *action steps* to de-stress. The more energy we have, the more we can accomplish. Stress uses energy. Therefore, the more stress we have, the more energy it takes to simply cope. If we are spending all our valuable resources managing the day-to-day grind, how can we create time and space for our creative thinking and dreams? It is vital for us to learn ways to de-stress, which increases energy. By harnessing our energy, we also maximize our vitality.

Quick stress reducers for maximizing creativity:

1. *Clear mind – with relaxation, breathing, meditation, stretching.*

2. *Physical exercise – walk, jog, yoga, swim.*

3. *Reach out – to a friend or family member you trust.*

4. *Laughter – enjoy a joke of the day, the comics or funny movie.*

5. *Look for inspiration – read books, go somewhere that inspires you.*

6. *Find gratitude – for the people and events that are causing you stress.*

Get a Balanced Perspective

We can increase vitality by changing our perspective on how we view the events that happen to us. It is with great certainty that I can say there will always be life events (good and bad) to deal with ranging from financial concerns to professional stressors to the death of loved ones. There are *pros and cons* to everything in life, even in crisis. When we find the gem in the crisis we also find peace and beauty. When we view life this way, it enables us to have a balanced perspective. This is one of the best ways to increase energy and our inner creative power.

Whenever you are feeling negative about anything at all, write down all the *pros and cons* of whatever is bothering you, whether you feel you made a wrong decision about something, a relationship that is bumpy or an emotion that is holding you back from pursuing an idea. Getting a balanced perspective by finding the *pros and cons* is a fast and effective means for our brains to come to decisions or conclusions, and to clear brain noise. Research shows the average person has *60,000 thoughts every day*. The more brain noise we have, the less time and energy we have to create. By writing out lists of the *pros and cons*, it allows us to clearly see what the benefits are of achieving what we set out to do and a great way to boost energy.

Exercise Regularly

There is no doubt that feeling tired or sluggish hampers creative energy. Whenever we are in a creative state of flow and begin to feel tired, it may be time to put on a pair of comfortable shoes and take a walk for some fresh air. *Walking* is one of the best ways to clear the mind, boost our energy and find inspiration. We can walk by ourselves, or ask a friend to join us for companionship and conversation.

A notch up from the walk is to jog, for those who are physically able. *Jogging* is a free way to exercise (be sure to have good runners) and is a great way of seeing neighbourhoods. Jogging can be quite enjoyable in beautiful surroundings such as parks and trail systems, and it can also foster inspiration.

Working out at a *gym or fitness centre* is ideal for those people who need to exercise with others to be motivated and who enjoy that kind of atmosphere. If you find you cannot get to a gym or organized classes, either because of time or budget limitations, there are a number of exercises you could do at home at your leisure – free-of-charge.

Simple exercises to do at home:

1. *Aerobic activity: walking, jogging, jump rope, step aerobics (with tapes)*

2. *Strengthening – use your own body weight to build muscles. Dumbbells and rubber tubes and balls are cheap and do not take up space. Try these for strengthening:*

   - *push ups*

   - *sit ups*

   - *bicep curls*

   - *overhead presses*

   - *triceps extensions*

   - *leg lifts (inner/outer thighs)*

   - *chair squats*

   - *calf raises*

3. Stretching – make sure your body is in alignment with strong abdominals and lower back muscles, and good posture. Try these stretches:

- *shoulder circles/static shoulder*

- *chest and back muscles*

- *high reaches with arms*

- *reach up/roll down*

- *standing quads*

- *calf stretch/hamstrings*

Pay Attention to Diet

It is imperative that we drink a lot of water every day to flush out toxins and keep our bodies hydrated and the mind sharp. There are some foods that can make us physically tired (some people are seriously affected by wheat and sugar), or foods that may give us allergic reactions we may not even realize. If we want to maximize our vitality, it is advisable to get on top of nutritional matters and have a healthy, balanced diet. For some, eating food that their body is intolerant to makes them lethargic; worse it can lead to serious illness. This obviously impacts the flow of creative juices.

Just a delicate word of caution about alcohol: it "numbs" emotions, therefore it also "numbs" creativity. As we all know, alcohol is a depressant and it can make one tired and lethargic. It puts the creative mind to sleep. Therefore, in order to maximize our vitality, to be as creative as we can be, consider curbing alcohol intake (for those that imbibe), especially when in a highly creative mode. To reach a higher level of creativity, it is critical that we allow ourselves to experience a wide range of emotions considered "normal," because we draw upon these emotions in our creative work. If we numb ourselves with alcohol, particularly on a regular basis, we do a disservice to our creativity.

Nutritional tips for maximizing creativity:

- *limit sugar (key)*
- *limit caffeine*
- *curb alcohol intake*
- *drink lots of water*
- *eat wholesome foods, where possible*
- *limit carbohydrates and fat*
- *take supplements, as appropriate*
- *check iron level regularly*

Sleep On It

"Sleeping on it" could very well be the key to the gift of *insight*. Throughout history, it has long been believed that sleep can stimulate creativity as well as scientific insight. Robert Louis Stevenson claimed to have written *The Strange Case of Dr. Jekyll and Mr. Hyde* from a dream. While sleeping, Samuel Taylor Coleridge was inspired to write the epic poem *Kubla Khan*. After dreaming about men with spears, inventor Elias Howe figured out where to put the eye of the needle in the design of the first sewing machine.

There is a popular story circulating that, in 1965, Paul McCartney woke up one morning to a tune playing in his head. Convinced he heard the tune elsewhere, he began searching for its origins until he realized the melody was…his own creation. *Yesterday* became one of the most played and recorded, and beloved, songs in music history.

A recent study by neurologists provides scientific proof that the gift of insight can occur while asleep. Researchers compared sleep to a form of offline processing for new memories. While asleep (one third of our lives are spent sleeping), mental glimpses of insight are reorganized into new, conscious knowledge.

Therefore take note of your sleeping patterns. The more hours we sleep, the less time we have to be creative in our waking hours. Conversely, if we do not get enough sleep it can dampen our creative energy. Maybe the answer, according to the research, is to get the right amount of sleep for you and it will fuel your creativity. Everyone is different. What is important is to be aware of the patterns.

One of my acquaintances works around the clock at a restaurant his family owns, yet he manages to spend time with his family, friends and play golf more than anyone I know. I asked him once if he ever sleeps. I found his reply intriguing: "I'll sleep when I'm dead," he said. I thought it was an interesting perspective to share.

Manage Time Efficiently Daily

Another way to increase vitality is to get organized and manage time effectively each and every day (taking into consideration the seven areas of life). It is called *Time Management*. A great way to start the day is to prioritize planned activities. When we feel good about our accomplishments, it adds to our energy, which helps our creativity.

Every morning, write out a "to do" list incorporating everything you need to accomplish for the day. You have a purpose for the day. Upon completion of each task, you will get satisfaction in stroking it off the page. At the end of the day, if you have accomplished everything you set out to do, it increases your energy and you will feel good about yourself.

On days when you feel you have not accomplished anything, or feel depressed, write out all the tasks you actually *did* accomplish. When you do this, you will see how productive you really were when you thought you were not. This can also help increase self-worth.

Try these time-saving ideas for creativity:

25 ways to make more room for creation every day:

1. Learn to multi-task around the house. Do "like" things at the same time.
2. Limit reading and sending e-mail until quiet times or at the end of the day.
3. Order groceries online. Limit visits to the grocery store to once a week.
4. Hire a housekeeper to clean at least once every two or three weeks.
5. Hire a dog walker or someone who can help take care of pets.
6. Do all banking online. Set up your account to automatically pay your monthly bills, so you do not have to think about it.
7. Take public transit wherever feasible. Getting stuck in traffic is a horrendous waste of time.
8. Limit watching television. Television is good for some informational and educational programming, but be aware of how much time it takes away from your productivity.
9. Limit surfing the Internet to what inspires you. There is so much cool information and entertainment on the Internet, but be aware of the time you spend.
10. Get take-out or pre-prepared food when really busy.
11. Go to the gym or workout in the early morning before the world wakes up. Read or listen to books on tape while you work out.
12. Delegate, delegate, delegate.
13. Read your daily newspaper online. Consider how much information is necessary and how much is not to limit the time you spending checking out the news of the day.
14. Consider renting if you own your house. This is a lifestyle choice, but there are benefits to not having to take the time to maintain a house/yard.
15. Shop only when you need to and for items you only really need.

16. Keep your workspace tidy and files organized.
17. Organize every morning with a "To Do" list and set priorities. Stroke off items as you go along. At the end of the day, write out all the tasks you accomplished that were not on the list.
18. Use voice mail whenever possible for imparting information rather than having a two-way conversation on the telephone.
19. Limit trips to the local coffee shop for that latte (if inclined).
20. Put away items in their proper place the first time, such as dishes, clothes and groceries.
21. Work or read in airports, while using public transportation and while waiting for people to arrive at meetings.
22. Listen to books on tape while driving around in your car for brain food. Turn what is otherwise unproductive time into valuable time.
23. For appointments, don't be late, don't be early, but be on time.
24. Get a cordless telephone that can be clipped to your clothing so you can talk on the phone while working and doing other household tasks.
25. Spend precious time with quality people that you love to be with, and not out of obligation.

Relaxation is the "Inspiring Ideas Incubator"

When we are relaxed, our ideas bake. When projects are not going as planned and our dream goes off the rails, take the cue that it is time to relax…go with the flow. We can find ourselves working against the grain creatively and it ends up being an uphill battle. If this happens, relax. There is a general misconception that relaxation equals wasting time. When it comes to creativity nothing can be further from the truth. In fact, this may be the time your creative genius kicks into gear.

Try several different methods of relaxing and find one or two that are best for you. *Yoga* works well and is good for us on a number of different levels. Take a yoga class or, if time is an issue, purchase yoga tapes and do the exercises at home on your own time. A long stroll in the park works wonders for relaxation. There are also many guided relaxation tapes that can be purchased at stores, or available free at the library.

Meditation is especially good for relaxation, even if it is for only 5-15 minutes per day. And it is free! As well, not wearing a watch may take some stress off. But if you decide to go without a watch, be mindful of not being late for appointments.

Spend Quality Time in Solitude

Even though we touched on this in an earlier section (*Be an Inspiring Person*), it is worth repeating here because it is important to increasing vitality. Spend quality time in solitude whenever possible. There is a time to be with others and a time to be alone. Clear a block of time for yourself every week (i.e. one day, or half-day) when you do not make unnecessary commitments to others and you are able to limit communication with the external world. Shut out the world so you can rejuvenate your spirit. If you have young children this may be challenging, but find a way to grab even a few hours to have that quality time in solitude to connect with your heart and soul.

We are all different, so discover what is best for you. If you explain to people why you need to disappear for a period of time, they will likely understand.

I live in that solitude which is painful in youth,
but delicious in the years of maturity.
-- Albert Einstein

Give These a Whirl:

1. *List 10 things that are stressful to you (i.e. having no money, teenaged children, relationships, pets, job, in-laws). Against each item, list ways to rid yourself of each stressor so you can free up your energy.*

2. *Take an inventory of your lifestyle: diet, sleeping patterns, relaxation techniques, time you spend alone and exercise routine. Ask yourself if you had even more energy than at present, how could this increased energy help your creativity? What would it do for you? After taking inventory, make any*

necessary adjustments. Change is generally good, so go for it! In if question, be sure to consult a physician about health matters.

3. *Consider a major decision you have to make. It could either be one in your personal or professional life. Make a list of all the pros and cons of this decision. Clear brain noise by writing it down, reviewing it, and seeing all the benefits and drawbacks.*

Spread Your Wings Beyond the Horizon

Einstein once said, "Imagination is more important than knowledge." Take a moment to ponder his words of wisdom.

If we desire to stretch ourselves creatively, we need to make a conscious effort *to spread our wings and broaden our horizons.* When we do this, we expand our minds, experiences, tastes and limits. The more we broaden our horizons in this world, the more we are able to develop and use our imagination. It is not only about developing the ole grey matter either, but rather it is about creating a total life experience.

Read Quality Books

One of the best ways to broaden yourself as a person is to *read.* We are what we read. Though do not read just anything at all: *read quality books.* Have a specific purpose for what you read. When we read with a purpose we are more focused and aligned with our goals, and not wasting precious time that could otherwise be used for creation. Read a variety of material because it adds depth as a creative person.

Most definitely read the classics, the books that have stood the test of time. By reading the classics, we connect with the writers and their stories that have inspired people around the world since their creation.

Spend time in bookstores absorbing accomplished authors and the ambitious neophyte writers alike. On a regular basis, try one of the gazillions of magazines on the newsstands that you have never read before. If you are on a budget, libraries are ideal resources for books and tapes/CDs, free-of-charge. As well, the Internet is full of all sorts of interesting reading material.

Tips to improve your reading:

- *Skim! You do not have to read every word printed in a magazine or book, including this one. This way, you get through more material in a shorter period of time.*

- *Take a speed-reading course. Some community colleges offer them.*

- *Every time you purchase a book or order one from the library, try a genre you have not read before (i.e mystery, romance, philosophy, religion, business, astrology, mythology, self-help, etc.).*

- *Challenge yourself and improve your level of reading.*

- *Be sure to give your eyes a rest now and again, and use sufficient light.*

- *Read classics by the great authors such as: Shakespeare, Leo Tolstoy, Jane Austen, Emily Brontë, H.G. Wells, Mark Twain, Lucy Maud Montgomery, Jonathon Swift. Study the classical works of Plato, Carl Jung, Einstein and other great scholars and thinkers.*

- *Above all, read with a purpose. This way you waste no time and you read material aligned with your values.*

Learn a New Language

Understanding another language, including Sign language for the deaf, helps to broaden our knowledge and skills. It allows us to communicate with people we otherwise might not have been able to. Knowing several languages also enables us develop tolerance of other cultures and in certain circumstances can prevent others from feeling isolated or lonely (consider the deaf). It adds depth as a creative person. Another beautiful reason to learn a new language is we increase our confidence and self-worth.

Many people I know say they want to learn a new language, but create all sorts of excuses for not doing it (myself included). The favourites are: no money and no time. These excuses are nothing more than that: excuses. Learning another language can be easy, practical and fun. If you wish to learn another language, make the time or find the funds. Make it happen. Why? It is an investment in yourself.

Learning a language can be easy, practical and fun:

1. *Listen to language lessons on tape while driving around in your car, doing housework or working out at the gym.*

2. *Start your mornings by memorizing a new phrase or two before dashing out the door to go to work.*

3. *Take a break at the office by practicing on a non-judgemental colleague.*

4. *Use your new language in social settings.*

5. *Enrol in a night course at a local college or community centre where you can share the experience with like-minded people.*

6. *Take a vacation in the country where the language is spoken; rejuvenate your spirit and learn at the same time.*

7. *Practice on your children or a pet. They can learn, too.*

When you are ready, consider taking on a foreign-speaking student to teach them about your first language (English or other). You learn about their language while you are at it. You will probably feel pretty good about yourself for doing it, too.

- *Do some research and learn to say "thank you" in several different languages, including Sign language. Commit it to memory and use these new words at any given opportunity.*

Did you know...

- *the French have only one way of expressing love: amour. In English, we often interchange "like" and "love," leaving everyone confused.*

- *Japanese is usually written vertically and from right to left.*

- *Gaelic has been spoken in Ireland for more than 2,000 years.*

- *Just as people who are able to hear use different languages in different countries, those who are deaf use different "Sign languages" to communicate in different parts of the world.*

Study the Sciences and Math

Studying the sciences may seem, well, counter intuitive for the creative mind. However, if we want to reach a higher level of creativity, it is valuable to have at least some knowledge of physics and quantum mechanics, chemistry, biology, as well as other sciences. I am inclined to also suggest becoming familiar with the "soft" sciences such as metaphysics and paraphysics (ESP). It is amazing to the point of mind-boggling to learn about how the body and the brain functions. Learning about the stars and the solar system flips a switch for the imagination. By studying geography we to get a bigger picture of the global village (travel is also valuable for this reason).

There is a good reason Leonardo da Vinci once expressed, "Study the science of art and the art of science." The sciences allow us to have a better understanding of the world we live in. We gain valuable perspective and open the creative mind. There can also be a lot of fun, experimentation and creativity involved in figuring out how things work.

Many people look to science to explain *spirituality*, including one of history's most scientific thinkers: Sir Isaac Newton. It is believed Newton was a Biblical expert who was motivated to explain gravity and invent calculus out of a desire to understand the mystery of creation and find "God's will" in nature. According to researchers, Newton prophesized the world would end violently in the year 2060, by using elaborate time charts based on his Biblical readings of *Daniel* and *Revelations*. Rather than sharing his prophecy, the great scientist and mystic kept it to himself. By today's standards, had he gone public with his views at that time, he would be considered a flake.

Remember Newton's apple? Let's revisit that example I used in the chapter *Ask Quality Questions*, of Newton observing the apple falling from the tree, while the moon hung in the sky, and asking himself...*why did the apple fall and not the moon, and does the same law that caused the apple to fall also apply to the moon?* Perhaps he was indeed asking a "quality question" aligned with the values of his whispering heart after all. In other words, maybe he wondered if the reason the apple fell and moon remained in the sky was connected with God, or if it explained God's will, apparently an important value to Newton. This may be the case of one of the most significant "quality questions" ever asked in history; one that revolutionized our world.

As far as *mathematics* (science's evil cousin) is concerned, it is valuable for us to sharpen our mathematics skills. I know, I know... you thought by leaving school you had put all that algebra homework behind you. Well, there is good reason for me to raise this. It may have never occurred to you, but mathematics is quite creative. Music, for instance, is closely connected to mathematics. Music in its purest form *is* mathematics. *Rhythm* and *pitch*, for example, are two primary musical concepts usually explained using mathematics. There is a lot of creativity and beauty in this connection.

- *To learn more about theories of how the Universe works through modern physics, pick up The Elegant Universe by Brian Greene, an illuminating, entertaining and easily understood book for non-physicists.*

135

Experience the World Through All Senses

The world is a smorgasbord. Allow yourself to indulge in the smorgasbord and open up to different ways of experiencing life through all of your senses. Our lives are enriched by experiencing the sights, sounds, tastes, scents and textures of our own culture, as well as other cultures -- from cuisine to music to sports to arts and crafts.

From my international travels, I recall the pungent spices wafting from food stalls in Bangkok, and the salty sea air brushing my nose when I first stepped off the airplane in the Caribbean. The image of the blue, blue sea against the crisp white buildings of Greece keeps me longing to return. In Venice, the taste of Italian ice cream while sitting in the piazza and watching beautiful people pass by. In Prague, the enchanting sound of classical music in palaces and churches, and on the streets. And the sweet voices of the tribal children in northern Thailand as they delightfully performed a traditional song and dance around the campfire. And the roar of chants and cheers of passionate soccer fans at a stadium in England, rousing my spirits with excitement. And the touch of the delicate woollen sweaters in the shops of Dublin, as well as the feel of the cool stone wall of the oldest church in Scandinavia.

These are but a few of my experiences that ignited my senses and have left an imprint on my mind and spirit forever, leaving me with a burning desire for more. These experiences also provided me with gems I use in my creative projects, whether they are ideas for stories or ways to decorate a room that I do my creative work in.

When we expand our horizons beyond our own backyards, our creativity expands. You do not even have to venture far if budget is tight. Check out the various multicultural neighbourhoods where you live. Check out the shops. Try a new restaurant for lunch or dinner and experiment with delicacies from around the world. Hang out with friends who are from a different cultural background and share their food, folk music, arts and crafts. Celebrate a traditional holiday with them and indulge your senses.

The world is a smorgasbord and we all bring a delightful dish to the table. Indulge with delight.

Dabble in the Arts

One of the quickest ways for us to open up our creativity is to dabble in the arts as much as possible. From the performing arts to visual arts to literature, we benefit from just hanging around it.

Music, especially, is amazing food for the soul. A universal language, music assists with learning, relaxation and creative thinking. It can also be healing. Whenever you have the chance attend concerts, whatever genre of music that suits your fancy. If money is tight, source out the local free performances.

Cultural events such as film festivals, authors' readings, dance performances and stage plays are terrific opportunities to experience the arts. Look for the pay-what-you-can performances. And check out free art galleries and studios.

When we resonate with a particular subject, we tend to value it more and want to share it with others. Dabbling in the arts opens up our creativity. Consider taking an art class, even if it is only for enjoyment or meeting people. If you are interested in developing your artistic talent, a "life drawing" course is a wise investment to build a foundation to springboard from. Put on your dancing shoes and take a dance class such as jazz or ballet. Or grab your partner and take a ballroom dance class, and the two of you share the experience together.

Expand your knowledge in the artistic areas of:

- *Opera and other classical music*

- *Water colours and oil painting*

- *Sculpture*

- *Modern and classical dance*

- *Film (writing, directing, set design, etc.)*

- *Photography*

- *Design*

Build a Personal Library

Although this was mentioned earlier in the book, it bears repeating: consider creating your own library or personal resource centre of books, movies and/or music. If you enjoy reading, there can be sheer pleasure in the process of collecting books on subjects that matter to you. If we are what we read, we must be the sum of all our books. It is the same for movies and music. Build a library you are proud of. It can take years to build a library, so do not feel badly if you have only started a collection. What is important is to just begin.

Games and Puzzles Aren't Just for Kids

As adults, we often take our work too seriously and forget to have fun for fun's sake. For many of us, fun equals being childish. Rubbish. Now and again, take a break from work with some *games* and *puzzles,* which are great tools to help tease and expand the mind…and have some sheer fun. All computers and cell phones come with games these days. Carry a Game Boy around in a briefcase and have some fun with it while zipping around in the back seat of a taxi on the way to your next meeting. Why not? Or rip out the crossword puzzle in the daily newspaper and give it a whirl.

While not as sexy as computer games, chess is a classic and one that has been known for ages to help develop problem-solving abilities. If this sounds too old-fashioned, there are computerized chess games on the market that you can play against the computer. It can be most challenging, intense and rewarding.

Engage your brain with some fun games and puzzles. By doing so, you expand your mind and may possibly even increase hand-eye coordination at the same time. We get enormous benefit by engaging in games and puzzles…they aren't just for kids!

Open yourself up to different ways of experiencing the world through all of your senses.

Spread Your Wings by Doing These:

1. *What subject would you like to learn more about (e.g. history, quantum physics, art, religion, spirituality, cooking, parenting, chess, a new language)? How could you incorporate that in your schedule? Are there classes you could take? Books you could read? Can you do it at home at your leisure? How would it serve you in getting where your heart is yearning to go?*

2. *Pick up a famous classic book (fiction or non-fiction). After you read it, ask yourself why you chose that particular book to begin with. What did you learn from it? Any important messages?*

3. *Spend a day enhancing all your senses: smell, taste, sight, hearing, touch and not to forget the sixth sense, intuition. Stretch your senses beyond your present limits. Try this when you are working on your creative projects. Make notes on how this sensory-enhancement impacts your creative energy or thinking.*

4. *On a quiet evening, instead of watching television (if you do) tease your brain with some puzzles or games. Try game and puzzle websites on the Internet. Pull out your old Scrabble, Monopoly or any other board game you may have hiding in a closet, blow of the dust and invite some friends over for some old-fashioned fun.*

Take Ideas to the End of the Line

I once read an article that quoted an advertising guru who said these wise words: "An idea has no value unless you do something with it." Although the name of the adman has since escaped me, these precious words never have.

Ideas can stay scribbled on scraps of paper, on our computers, or tucked away in our brains forever. There is value, of course, in having gone through the creative process to dream up the idea to begin with. However, there is even *more* value when our ideas become reality. Taking it a step further, once you have an idea, how can you make it bigger and even *more* valuable than you initially thought? How far could you push it? Take ideas to the end of the line and see how far your wings take you.

If you already have an idea, what could you do to further expand it? How can you make it a reality? What can you do to exhaust all its possibilities and make it bigger than big? For example, let's say you had an idea for a new brand of home-cooked organic food for dogs. Think of the infinite possibilities for the new brand. How could you push that idea to the end of the line?

When exploring an idea or concept, do not be Ms. or Mr. *Lazy Pants* and stop at the first notion or solution you come up. Keep going! The same thought applies when solving a problem, whether it is a personal or business matter. Exhaust all possibilities for your ideas. Push ideas to the max.

Get Different Angles on Ideas

One way to push the limits is to take an idea and look at it from every possible angle. Flip it upside-down, turn it inside-out. *Get several different angles on an idea*. The way to do this is to examine the idea based on a variety of perspectives.

Using our organic dog food as an example, how could we get different angles on the idea of producing, marketing and distributing such as product? Well, it is logical to begin by determining who is interested in buying or using this product and use that information as a jumping off point. What would these potential customers be like? What are their interests? Are there other animals that would benefit from this food? Are cats likely to go wild for it? What do vets have to say about it? How could you market such a product? If you dislike dogs, what would you say about this product? If dogs could cook, what would a dog cook *for you*? And so forth. Start off logically, then go wild.

As you can see, by engaging in this kind of creative thinking we can get a number of different takes on an idea, which enables us to further expand and explore our vision.

Map Out Your Vision

Mapping out your vision or ideas in a visual way on paper is a brilliant method of developing and exploring ideas and concepts that is non-linear and non-limiting. You start by writing the "main idea" (or seed of the vision) in the middle of a piece of paper and then draw branches (approximately 6-8) out from it with the "key associated words" or "associated thoughts" that fall out of your main idea. From every branch you further explore "associated words" or "associated thoughts" of the word on that particular branch…and so on. By mapping out your idea visually to expand and explore your vision, you make wonderful "connections." When you have completed it, the whole thing ends up looking sort of like a tree.

Try this method for business planning, preparing presentations and developing stories. Use colourful markers to spice it up visually. By mapping out ideas using this visual way of connecting "key associated words or thoughts," the notion is this: the possibilities for our ideas are *infinite* because we can make endless connections. For more detailed information, check out Tony Buzan's book *The Power of Creative Intelligence*, which explores this concept in stunning visual detail. Michael Gelb's book *How to Think Like Leonardo da Vinci* also covers this concept visually.

Brainstorm Ideas

Alex Osborne, the quintessential adman and pioneer of *brainstorming*, once declared, "It's easier to tone down a wild idea than to think up a new one." Brainstorming is an effective and time-efficient way to generate ideas and further develop existing ones. Toss around ideas with a group of friends, family members or colleagues in a "power think tank." See how your ideas grow…and how quickly.

In the world of marketing, public relations and advertising, brainstorming is used on a regular basis to quickly and effectively generate marketing and communication ideas and business solutions for companies and products. Based on my experience, if you aim to have an effective brainstorming session there are a few general guidelines to keep in mind:

Brainstorming guidelines:

- *Find a quiet, comfortable space.*

- *Limit the session to one hour otherwise participants fall asleep.*

- *Choose a group manageable in size (approximately 3-10 people).*

- *Give participants an incentive to attend your brainer, such as free pizza and beer, in return for an hour of their time. Keep in mind the law of fair exchange: they, too, must get something from the experience.*

Get Into the Head of Someone You Admire

Okay, I realize this one may sound corny, but I sometimes find this exercise quite useful when I am on an ideas fishing expedition. Using your imagination, jump into the head of a mentor, role model or anyone else you admire. They can be a person in your life right now or someone famous or even fictitious. By doing this exercise, you look at your idea through *their point of view.* You ask yourself what they might hypothetically say about your idea. This is one way of helping to max out ideas.

Think of any idea you have – any idea at all. Then envision what someone famous might say about it such as Oscar Wilde, Winston Churchill, Ray Charles, Bono or Einstein. Or try a movie character like the Lord of the Ring's character Frodo. By getting into their head, you may gain some valuable perspective. If nothing else, it can be a cheap and fun source of entertainment.

Technology as a Creative Tool

Love it or hate it, we live in a wired, technological world and *technology* itself can be used as a creative tool. Digital pianos, cameras and computers are all advanced technological tools used for creative purposes. Professionals such as graphic designers, animators, writers, publishers, filmmakers, television producers, marketers and photographers all rely on technology.

I wrote this book using technology. The book cover was designed using technology. It was printed using technology. It got into your hands thanks to technology.

Technology can also be used to explore and expand creative thinking. There are a number of technological methods that enable us to max out ideas. The Internet is an enormously powerful and fast means of exploring and doing research. Look into the various software programs available on the market to help generate and develop ideas, or organize your time to be more creative for that matter. Depending on your interests and needs there are a range of programs on the market to assist with writing, music composing, graphic design, publishing and photography. The Internet is also loaded with "how to" websites. Check it out.

If you happen to be techno-phobic, which many people are, and you have a burning desire to use a technical program such as music composing or desktop publishing, all you have to do to transcend this fear is take bite-sized action steps to learn the skills. You can do it! Take a course. Buy a book. Go to your local computer store and ask questions. Find someone who is savvy with the technology you wish to learn and ask them for guidance, or hire their services. Take it from a former techno-dweeb…it is really not that daunting. Honest. All that is required is the desire and the courage to take the first step to learn the necessary skills and you are well on your way to becoming accomplished. Who knows,

143

you could very well become the next big rock star!

Discover Quick Ways to Generate New Ideas.

Need to start from the beginning? Here are a few ways to quickly generate new ideas.

8 Quick ways of dreaming up new ideas:

1. *Gather ideas from real life stories by reading newspapers and magazines, listening to the radio and watching the news on television.*

2. *Think of two or three people in your life and link them in unusual ways to create fictional stories or come up with What If scenarios.*

3. *Read a classic novel and turn it into a modern story, either literature, film or radio; a story that is relevant for today's audiences.*

4. *Write down the dreams you have while sleeping – good and bad – explore and expand them.*

5. *Look at your own life with a fresh new twist, one that inspires you.*

6. *Think of a big lesson you had in life. Expand on it. Look at it from various perspectives. What is the moral of the story? What can others learn from it?*

7. *See the world through the eyes of a child and develop your ideas from that vantage point.*

8. *Recall your "firsts" in your adolescent years, like the first time you drove a car, got a job, made love, travelled alone, got a "pad" with a roommate.*

A highly creative mind maximizes all the possibilities for ideas. By pushing the boundaries of the mind -- our ideas grow. No matter what the outcome, whether our ideas take off or flame out, consider it a valuable learning experience. When we endeavour to push our ideas to the end of the line, just by engaging in the creative process itself, our wings lift us up and take us to places we have never been. And we learn about ourselves and increase our self-worth along the way.

Push ideas to the max.

Give These a Whirl:

1. *Make a list of 5 well-known people that you admire (author, world leader, philosopher, movie star or movie character). They could be living or deceased. Then write a sentence or two about what your idea or creative project is, or a way of life you would love to live. Against each of the five names, write down what you believe each of those 5 well-known people might say about your idea or desire. Think long and hard about their viewpoint. Once you have completed this, determine how you can use the information.*
2. *Spend time surfing the Internet to explore the many different sites that can help expand your ideas. Type ideas on a search engine and see where it takes you. Use it as a source for inspiration.*

The Power of Sexual Energy

Love is the extremely difficult realization
that someone other than oneself is real.
-- Iris Murdoch

Sexual energy and creative energy are so strongly connected that they impact each other profoundly – this is pure biology, chemistry and physics in cahoots with one another.

There is no doubt sexual tension affects our passion, energy and productivity. When we learn to harness and properly channel our sexual energy, we get the fuel to keep our creative motors running. With this in mind, I cannot think of a better reason to be indulging in wine, oysters, chocolates, lingerie, cologne and scented candles…why not? Aphrodisiacs boost creativity. Honest!

Think about the time when you first met your spouse, a new flame or the hot guy/girl you bumped into while on vacation, and how you had energy and passion that drove you wild. *Sexual energy fuels inspiration and passion, and when harnessed and properly channelled is a pleasurable and powerful means to motivate us creatively.*

Some professional athletes avoid sex at least 24 hours prior to competition, so they can harness their pent-up sexual energy for that important game. The ancient Greek athletes (originally only men were allowed to compete) were so serious about the Olympic championships they did not touch a woman, or another man, for at least one week prior to their game in order to keep the "inner flame" lit.

People who work together and are physically attracted to each other are usually more productive because there is a "charge" that fuels their creative energy. It can be an electrical experience reaping amazing results. Consider the number of soap operas and primetime dramas on television (e.g. *ER, General Hospital, Boston Legal, The Practice*) that are built on this dynamic. And chances are you probably know of someone (friend, family member or colleague) who married a person they met while working together.

According to Napoleon Hill, author of the classic book *Think and Grow Rich,* which was based on his research of the keys to success of American's rich and famous men, "the average man reaches his greatest capacity to create between the ages of forty and sixty." The reason, he states, is because that is the time in life when *harnessing and channelling sexual energy* is learned.

Some people claim they become more sexually aroused when feeling especially creative or when working on a project. However, when we are in a "highly charged" state of creativity, or an extreme state of flow, our sex drive may actually wane for a period of time. This happens when a creative project becomes the centre of our world and we dedicate all attention and energy into making it happen. When we are in this groove, sex often takes a back seat – or falls off the radar screen entirely.

Historically, it has been noted that some of the great "master" creative geniuses, such as Michelangelo (who was known to have extremely light sleeping patterns), abstained from sex for long periods of time while they worked on their masterpieces around the clock. "What if"… these masters had not harnessed and channelled their sexual energy? It's quite possible they would not have given birth to their masterpieces that inspire us today, such as Michelangelo's David. Or we would have something completely or radically different to be inspired by.

Many artists over the centuries and across many cultural eras have embraced or used their sexual energy and turned it *into* their art. How many times have you seen the image of the female and male physique represented in paintings, photographs, sculptures, sketches and so forth? Next time you go into an art museum, check out the way human sexuality is represented in art or has influenced art throughout history.

For example, Henri de Toulouse-Lautrec, who became famous as the bohemian artist of the Moulin Rouge, captured the spirit and emotion of the belle époque (the "beautiful era") in Paris through his art. The Moulin Rouge, which was a theater and concert and dance hall all in one, was the place where one would find Lautrec nightly at the same table sketching (and drinking) whatever suited his fancy…especially the dancers. Those images of the Moulin Rouge are now part of art history.

And so, our sexual energy can be used to help keep our creative engines running. However, the problem lies when we give sex far too much attention and energy. Just like any other numbing agent, such as

147

alcohol, drugs and food, using too much of our sexual energy diffuses our creative energy and therefore decreases our creative power. It simply takes the focus off our creative projects. Of course, with anything else in life, balance is usually best.

There is nothing either good or bad but thinking makes it so.
-- Shakespeare

Consider These:

1. *Can you recall a time when hanging out with a special person made you more creative and even wildly productive? A time when you jumped out of bed earlier than usual, did your damnedest to look great, had a hop in your step all day...and did a week's worth of work in a few hours.*

2. *Experiment with your sexual energy over the next few weeks and see how it impacts your creative thinking. Engage your partner in the experimentation and see how it impacts your relationship and other areas of your life. How does it impact your partner's creativity?*

Earn a Living By Doing What You Love

The more you give, the more good things come to you.
-- Crow proverb

You may have never thought of money in this way, but money is an *energy system*. The energy you give out to the world comes back to you as *money energy*. The more people you touch with your energy (i.e. services, business, inspiration, teaching, etc.) the more *money energy* comes back.

The simplest way of understanding how money energy works is this: money goes to people who value it and those who put energy into having it.

How do you view money? Do you value having money? Or do you value money only when you *don't* have it?

If you want to have money it must be listed as one of your top core values. If you want prosperity, you must think about being prosperous. If you like the concept of having money in the bank, but deep down feel it is not within your reach, then it is time to change the way you view money. Since energy flows where attention goes, start thinking *green* -- the colour of money.

The best method of having a life of prosperity is this: devote time and energy to making money by doing what you love, whether it is making art, playing music, developing a new business, a hobby or teaching a subject matter dear to your heart. You have probably come across this advice in other self-help books or heard it said by famous experts and motivational speakers many times before. Well, there is a good reason for it.

When we are doing what we love, we feel joyful and fulfilled, and are able to find the time and energy to continue doing more of it. Exercise your creativity and find a way to make money. Explore all of your creative abilities and develop a variety of income streams. Taking it a step further, how could you turn your idea, creative project or hobby into a high-performing money-making machine that, in turn, could help other people make money? Make it the gift that keeps on giving.

The key to having a prosperity mind-set is to believe that financial rewards are really achievable and, as if by magic, they come to you. *Believing* is seeing, not the other way around. We all have the ability to achieve financial rewards. I can think of countless examples of famous people who have made enormous achievements in the finance department, but the start of their journey was something quite different.

- *Walt Disney arrived in Hollywood with $40 and a suitcase of clothes. Look how far his $40 went.*

- *Bill Gates and Paul Allen did not have the funds to start a software company. Today, who is not touched by the world's largest software company?*

- *Oprah Winfrey grew from humble roots in rural Mississippi into a legacy as one of the most important and influential people in modern times.*

- *J.K. Rowling was a single mother with little income when she wrote the manuscript for Harry Potter. Today, with several Harry Potter books and movies behind her, she is reportedly a billionaire. A financial success phenomenon.*

Now, I recognize that not everyone sets out to have a life of riches or financial success; especially people who choose to work in artistic fields. And that is okay. There are many artists I know who claim to be "purists" because they do not create their art for commercial purposes or financial gains, but purely for the noble love of it. And that is okay. Some of these artists choose to live in poor conditions because of this belief. Unfortunately, this belief perpetuates the "starving artist" stereotype. This way of thinking may seem noble to some, but it is not realistic in today's fast-paced, adrenaline-pumping, commercial-oriented world.

This is when it is time to face the facts: it is difficult to have a good quality of life without earning an income. If you have the desire, skills and the know-how to earn a decent living from your creative endeavours or abilities or ideas, it is wise to do so. You can do it! Honest! I cannot imagine a more enjoyable way of earning a living than by doing what we love to do. Besides, if you are able to create something that has commercial value, and someone else is willing to pay you handsomely for it, why not?

Find a way to earn a living by doing what you love and what brings joy to your life. While you are at it, use this simple money-making *philosophy* and you will see how easily achievable financial rewards are:

Money-making philosophy for the creative dreamer:

Desire to generate income from your ideas.
Ask for what you want; and never be afraid to ask for help.
Believe in yourself, your ideas and your earning power.
Give it your best shot.
Achieve financial rewards and success as a result.

Desire – Ask – Believe – Give -- Achieve

Tips on turning your idea into a money-making machine:

1. *Make the desire for prosperity (or "wealth") one of your top values.*

2. *Come up with an idea that has commercial appeal.*

3. *Look at a variety of ways to make money based on your idea, or creative abilities.*

4. *Do not put limits on yourself.*

5. *Develop a solid business and marketing plan.*

6. *Connect with people who can further develop your idea, help generate business leads and connect you with potential*

investors and financial lenders.

7. *Consider strategic partnerships, especially if resources are limited. Look for people who complement areas where you feel you lack expertise.*

8. *Study money. Read books on the power of earning money, investing and financial planning.*

9. *Learn the secrets of highly successful sales persons and marketers, and adapt their strategies.*

10. *Devote the time to make money.*

11. *Get support from family and friends.*

12. *Never be afraid to ask for what you want.*

13. *Pay no attention to people who pooh-pooh your idea or projects.*

14. *Do what you love and love what you do.*

15. *Believe in yourself.*

If you need to *save* more money in order to get your creative project off the ground, or see it through to the end, try these money saving suggestions to fund your project:

10 Money Savers to help fund your creative dreams:

1. *Expand your earning potential using your creative abilities in multiple ways (various streams of income) so you can save more money. Get a second job if you have to. Or if you are self-employed, pick up another contract or additional piece of business.*

The Whispering Heart

2. *Sell some assets to tide you over until you earn a living doing what you love.*

3. *Rent an apartment or house rather than owning the property. If you sell your property, invest the money to make more money. Depending on where you live and your lifestyle, the case may be the opposite.*

4. *Consider making changes or adjustments to your lifestyle.*

5. *Shop at dollar stores for materials such as notepads, markers, crayons, etc.*

6. *Check out what your local community centre has for courses (drawing, dance, language) that are free-of-charge.*

7. *Pay attention to junk mail and e-mails offering specials. You would be surprised what you can save by taking notice of the junk you get.*

8. *For every paycheque you get automatically put a portion of it, such as 10 per cent, into a "creative dream" bank account or mutual fund.*

9. *Develop a budget, and limit your spending on meals and entertainment.*

10. *Spend according to your values.*

Help other people get what they want –
and you'll get what you want.
-- Mary Kay Ash

Give These a Whirl:

1. *Write out a list of all the things you could do or buy if you had all the money in the world. Exhaust the list. Spend hours if you must. Do this exercise until you get excited about all the possibilities. Once you are excited, it will give you a kick-start to finding ways to achieving more prosperity in your life, and ways to fund your dreams.*

2. *Revisit the list of your top core values you did in the chapter The Balancing Act: Seven Areas of Life. Does "wealth" or "prosperity" appear on your list and, if so, in what order does it appear on the list? In other words, how much of a priority have you given having money in your life? If you want wealth or prosperity, it should be listed as one of your top three core values.*

Check In With Your Whispering Heart

Helped are those who create anything at all,
for they shall relive the thrill of their own conception.
-- Alice Walker

As human beings living in modern times, we become so busy with work, social activity, family obligations, financial challenges and our own brain noise, that we get into the "doing" mode and forget to pause and ask ourselves if we are experiencing joy. Or we get so caught up in the passion and magic of our creation that we stop being realistic about our expectations and outcomes, and how it impacts our well-being, or the well-being of loved ones.

For your creativity's sake, now and again pause and reflect upon your dream. Do a complete systems analysis of your mind, body and spirit. When you close this book, when we finish our journey together, please do a "time out" and connect with your whispering heart. Ask yourself quality questions, but be patient if the answers do not appear immediately. They *will* come. Try asking yourself these kinds of questions: Is your creative dream still connected to the values of your heart? Are you enjoying the creative process? Do you need to make any changes? Is this creative dream still important to you? Do you feel joy? Are there obstacles holding you back from joy and fulfillment? What can you do to remove those obstacles? How could you make a living from your creativity?

Now and again, as you continue your journey on your own, take the time to check in with your whispering heart. Listen to the wisdom it offers. The heart tells us the truth and there is always an "inner knowing" of what is right for us. The heart knows if we are resonating with our creative aspirations and congruent with our goals, just like the heart knows if we are with the right mate. The heart knows if we are in the right job or line of business. Your heart knows if the life decisions you make are the best for you.

When we ask our heart what is best for us and beg for the answer, there is something magical about what happens next -- the right answer appears. Once we get the right answer, and really connect with it, we need to honour the answer with honesty...and make decisions accordingly. Then, and only then, are we able to have the most joyful life possible filled with creative expression and freedom. By honouring your heart and listening to the wisdom it whispers, it will serve you well.

We can get hell-bent on an idea and put all our energy into it, but there are times when it wanes and we lose interest. Inevitably, our precious baby disappears into the ozone. Sound familiar? These are the times when we have to try a different route. Know it is okay to do this and it is part of the process. Ask your heart quality questions and you shall receive quality answers that guide you on your journey.

If obstacles become insurmountable and we hit a dead end after trying *every* route possible, perhaps it is time to let the dream go...and move on...and get a new one. Though we should never lose sight that nothing in life is easy; things that come easy are not likely worthwhile. The same thing applies to our creative endeavours. We are likely in it for the long haul, so it is good to determine if your creative dream has sticking power to see you through to the end.

At some point during the process, we need to decide if we should put a foot on the accelerator -- or the brake. No matter the outcome, what is important is to feel proud of whatever ideas you had, actions you took and all that you learned throughout the process. Give yourself a well-deserved pat on the back.

Sometimes we hit a wall because we worry (fear) whether we are able to earn a living by pursuing our ideas and following our dreams. When we are so wrapped up in fear about whether or not money is coming in the door, we begin to question if our creative dreams are really important to us. Or we outright quit our dreams because we do not believe they can, or ever will, pay the bills.

Well, you *can* earn a living doing what you love. As we covered earlier, but bears repeating...money is an energy system. Energy flows where attention goes. Whatever you put your energy into, it pays back dividends. If you believe in yourself enough, you can and will find a way to earn a living from your creativity and doing what you love. Believe and you shall receive. At the end of the day we have to pay the bills. With this in mind, it is by far more enjoyable earning a living by doing what we love to do.

Lastly, know that creativity moves in a cycle like a wave. Enjoy the *up* cycle and learn from the *down* cycle. Remember, regardless of whether your creative project gets off the ground, or becomes a smashing hit, you benefit by the experience alone. Throughout the process, you will have transcended self-doubt, increased your self-worth, connected with the wisdom of your whispering heart and learned a lot about life and yourself along the way. Sounds like a beautiful gift to me.

Creativity moves in a cycle like a wave.
Enjoy the up cycle and learn from the down cycle

Alas, we are at the end of our journey together. This is the last exercise, I promise.

Please revisit the commitment you made to yourself at the start of this book, about committing to your creative dream. You may have experienced a change of heart after reading this material. Or perhaps you have expanded your creative dream, or may have added many others. Please take the time to write down your commitment to yourself once again. I know this may seem corny, but there is something magical about writing down our ideas and dreams, and committing to them. It brings the intangible (abstract) into the tangible (material) world, and makes it real.

Like your creative dream.

The heart to conceive, the understanding to direct,
and the hands to execute.
-- Junius

16 Action Steps to Unlock Your Creative Power: Summary Snapshot

In this final section, I have summarized the key points of the book into 16 "action steps" to unlocking your creative power and making all your dreams come true.

1. Ignite Inspiration

- Discover what inspires you – find the passion
- Connect with inspiring people
- Learn about famous "creatives"
- Be self-motivated
- Consider collaborating on projects, or join a special interest group
- Get a mentor(s); then eventually take on a student
- Be inspired from the heart, which leads to creation
- Connect with nature
- Visit museums, art shows, galleries, theatres and other cultural places
- Make your home and workplace environments "wow" inspirational
- Get sparked by sports or recreational activities
- Be aware of "connections" around you

2. Be an Inspiring Person

- Strive to live with an open heart by finding love and gratitude for the people and events in your life
- Transcend negative feelings, which lead to or foster self-doubt.
- Believe in yourself by increasing self-worth
- Discover your life's purpose (what gives you joy and meaning)
- Identify strengths and weaknesses; turn weaknesses into strengths

- Spend quality time alone
- Record heart whispers in a notebook or on tape
- Project a good self-image and think/speak like an inspiring person
- Meditate in a way best for you
- Incorporate prayer into your daily routine
- Visualize the life you desire
- Expand your consciousness and think big
- Listen to intuition
- Own your intention and take responsibility for your dreams
- Do your best; strive for excellence
- Be patient and gain wisdom
- Follow your whispering heart

3. Surround Yourself with Challengers and Champions

- Surround yourself with people who challenge and support you
- Conversely, be aware of the negative energy of Fire-Breathing Dragons and Energy Vampires, and limit your exposure to them

4. Use Your Whole Brain

- Learn to use your whole brain
- Whole brain thinking uses both the analytical and the creative sides equally well, accessing both sides of the brain's hemisphere at the same time
- Working on a computer and playing the piano are ways to develop whole brain thinking

5. Be Colourful

- Use colour to enhance your environment, wardrobe and mood
- Learn how colour affects you personally (each person is different)

6. Give Your Life A Shake!

- Challenge rules
- Be willing to destroy in order to create
- Be open to positive transformation and change
- Mix up your daily routine
- Travel, even if it's around the neighbourhood
- Turn off the phone, e-mail, pager occasionally
- Laugh as much as possible
- Open your mind to other ways of living and doing everyday things
- Be spontaneous and flexible
- Identify and overcome unwanted or unhealthy patterns
- Develop patterns that are beneficial

7. Live with Courage, Take Risks

- Live with courage
- Live by the mantra: Out of my zone of comfort lies my destiny
- Risk-taking is directly linked to your self-worth
- Challenge yourself; set small goals to begin with
- Believe in yourself
- When your certainty is greater than the doubt of others, or your own doubt, your certainty will rule (certainty > doubt)
- See the pros and cons of any risks you may take
- Do not take NO for an answer – persevere

8. Take the View that it's All a Learning Experience

- There is no such thing as mistakes – only lessons
- Let go of the fear of making mistakes
- Learn your lessons and gain wisdom
- Overcome obstacles
- Persistence is key
- Trust the creative process
- As long as your project is in your heart, do not give up until

going forward becomes futile
- It's all a learning experience

9. Ask Quality Questions

- The quality of questions you ask yourself and others determines the quality of your life
- Ask "What If" questions
- Be curious and inquisitive
- Hang around quality people

10. Balance Your Life: Seven Areas

- Balance your time and energy in the seven areas: career, finance, mental, social, spiritual, family and physical
- This will give you more energy for creativity
- Spending too much time and energy in one area will negatively impact another, so balance is best

11. Increase Vitality

- Be healthy -- maximize vitality
- Reduce stress
- Get a balanced perspective
- Exercise regularly
- Pay attention to diet
- Sleep on it
- Harness energy and balance lifestyle (seven areas)
- Manage time efficiently
- Relaxation is the "Inspiring Ideas Incubator"
- Spend quality time in solitude

12. Spread Your Wings Beyond the Horizon

- Broaden horizons and expand your mind
- Read quality books, especially the classics
- Learn a new language

- Study the sciences, including the "soft" sciences, and math
- Experience the world through all senses
- Dabble in the arts
- Build a library or other personal resource centre (books, films, music)
- Tease the mind with games and puzzles

13. Take Ideas to the End of the Line

- Push ideas to the max
- Flip ideas upside-down, turn ideas inside-out
- Visually explore/map out ideas and your vision
- Brainstorm to power think ideas
- Get into the head of someone you admire to get different perspectives on ideas
- Use technology as a tool for creativity purposes and to expand ideas
- Discover quick ways of generating new ideas
- Exhaust all possibilities for your ideas and make them big

14. Use the Power of Sexual Energy

- Learn to harness and properly channel sexual energy and it will fuel your creative engine

15. Earn a Living By Doing What You Love

- Devote time to making money by utilizing your creative abilities and doing what you love to do
- Turn your idea or creative project into a money-making machine
- Believe that financial rewards are achievable and they come to you
- Make prosperity one of your top 3 values
- Money-making philosophy: Desire, Ask, Believe, Give, Achieve
- Find ways to save money to fund your creative dream

16. Check In With Your Whispering Heart

- Pause and reflect on your dream now and again
- Connect with your whispering heart that guides you
- Does your idea have sticking power?
- Decide to stop or go
- Find ways to earn a living by what you desire
- Creativity moves in a cycle like a wave: enjoy the *up* cycle and learn from the *down* cycle
- Make a commitment to yourself

Parting Words

Writing this little book was an enlightening and enriching journey for me. I learned some valuable lessons, doors of opportunity opened like magic, and I made all sorts of "connections" with fascinating and successful people. A world of possibilities unfolded before my eyes.

Admittedly, when I first came up with the concept for the book I thought to myself, "Who am I to believe I can inspire others?" I had other nasty thoughts like, "What if it stinks?" The best one of all, "Who in their right mind would want to read *my* book?" Like any other creative human being, self-doubt thoughts reared their ugly heads.

The advantage I had that kept me going through the process was this: a back pocket filled with handy tools to fix the problems and design the solutions. A wrench to squeeze the life out of self-doubt; a hammer to smash in the face of fear; duct tape to gag the guilt; a saw to cut away resentment; bandages for the scrapes from the unforeseen falls; a ladder for the highs; power tools for drilling positive affirmations into my psyche; and balls of cotton to protect the gratitude deep within my heart. All the tools necessary to convince me that, indeed, I had the know-how to complete my own personal creative project so that I could in turn share with others the keys to creative achievement, and therefore a life filled with joy and fulfillment.

Those tools are between these two book covers. They work magic for me and I am certain they will work magic for you, too.

In closing, my deepest gratitude to *you* for picking up this little book, sticking it out to the last page and being with me every step of the way. May you find bliss along your journey, wherever your whispering heart takes you.

-- Shannon

The reward of a thing well done is to have done it.
-- Ralph Waldo Emerson

Creativity Resources and Inspirational Reading

Interested in learning more? I personally recommend reading these books on topics ranging from inspiration to wisdom to vitality to creative thinking.

- ***How to Think Like Leonardo da Vinci: Seven Steps to Genius Every Day** (Michael Gelb)*

  - an eclectic look at an eclectic super-human

- ***Think and Grow Rich** (Napoleon Hill)*

  - a timeless inspirational book for achieving success

- ***A Whack on the Side of the Head** (Roger von Oech)*

  - a humorous look at creative thinking

- ***Lateral Thinking** (Edward de Bono)*

  - any book by the popular master of creative thinking, de Bono, is worth a read

- ***The Artist's Way and Walking in This World** (Julia Cameron)*

  - these popular books are a definite read to help creatives unblock

- ***How Much Joy Can You Stand?** (Suzanne Falter-Barns)*

  - a whimsical and inspirational read about making your dreams come true, which I whole-heartedly enjoyed

- ***The Power of Creative Intelligence** (Tony Buzan)*

  - a great little book on the method of exploring ideas and concepts visually

- ***12 Secrets of Highly Creative Women*** *(Gail McMeekin)*

  - inspirational stories of women who used their creativity to achieve success

- ***You are Loved*** *(Dr. Lise Janelle)*

  - an insightful read on developing good self-worth and following the wisdom of one's heart; the basis of some of the principles presented in this book

- ***The Four Agreements*** *(Don Miguel Ruiz)*

  - an inspiring book based on ancient Toltec wisdom

- ***Eating Well for Optimum Health*** *(Dr. Andrew Weil)*

  - a popular book by a popular doctor about eating for health

- ***The Elegant Universe: Superstrings, Hidden Dimensions and the Quest for the Ultimate Theory*** *(Brian Greene)*

  - an entertaining voyage through modern physics toward an understanding of how the Universe works, including superstrings, hidden dimensions and more. Not for the faint of heart, mind you.

- ***Practical Intuition: How to Harness the Power of Your Instinct and Make it Work for You*** *(Laura Day)*

  - interesting insights into intuition…neat exercises!

- ***Molecules of Emotion: The Science Behind Mind-Body Medicine*** *(Candace Pert)*

  - Neuroscientist Dr. Candace Pert proves the mind and the body are not two separate entities, but one interconnected information system

- ***The Mozart Effect: Tapping the Power of Music to Heal the Body, Strengthen the Mind and Unlock the Creative Spirit*** *(Don Campbell)*

  - an exploration of music and how it impacts us

Inspiring Quotes

What follows are additional proverbs and words of wisdom geared toward inspiring creative thinking. Ponder them. Say them aloud. Paste them somewhere in your house, such as a bathroom mirror, fridge, in a notebook, on a bulletin board or above your computer. Use these words of wisdom as a means to encourage you to keep marching toward your dream.

What we play is life.
-- Louis Armstrong

Every child is an artist. The problem is how to remain an artist once he grows up.
-- Pablo Picasso

Nothing has a stronger influence psychologically on their children than the unlived life of the parent.
-- Carl Jung

True life is lived when tiny changes occur.
-- Leo Tolstoy

Only when he no longer knows what he is doing does the painter do good things.
-- Edgar Degas

Paint the essential character of things.
-- Camille Pissarro

It is what we fear that happens to us.
-- Oscar Wilde

Everything is miraculous. It is a miracle that one does not melt in one's bath.
-- Pablo Picasso

My soul can find no staircase to Heaven unless it be through Earth's loveliness.
-- Michelangelo

There is no love when there is no will.
-- Mohandas K. Gandhi

All our knowledge has its origin in our perceptions.
-- Leonardo da Vinci

Don't let yesterday use up too much of today.
-- Cherokee proverb

The more you ask how far you have to go, the longer your journey seems.
-- Seneca proverb

When one door of happiness closes, another opens; but often we look so long at the closed door that we do not see the one which has opened for us.
-- Helen Keller

The lowest ebb is the turn of the tide.
-- Henry Wadsworth Longfellow

We are such stuff as dreams are made of.
-- Shakespeare, A Midsummer Night's Dream

Those who want the fewest things are nearest to the gods.
-- Socrates

The more you know, the less you understand.
-- Tao Te Ching

When it blows, the mountain wind is boisterous, but when it blows not, it simply blows not.
-- Emily Brontë

Author's Workshops and Website

For more information and a schedule of workshops on inspiration and creativity, lectures and other inspirational materials by Shannon Skinner, please visit us at www.createwithjoy.com, or her weblog at www.whisperingheart.typepad.com. Or e-mail the author at sskinner@sympatico.ca.

About the Author

SHANNON SKINNER is a communication consultant, coach, author and filmmaker. She has designed creative communication programs for numerous distinguished companies. As a writer she has published short fiction and articles, and has also written screenplays. She has producing credits in both independent film and television. She also leads workshops on inspiration and creativity, and has taught marketing public relations at Ryerson University. She lives in Toronto.

Printed in the United States
39170LVS00002B/7-54

9 780973 761504